Like his seminars and himself, Robert's book positively glows with energy and power. It is a joy to experience and absorb. Reading this book empowers me and nurtures me. I believe it will do the same for you. We need this book. The more people who read it, the happier life will be.

--William Park, President, Hearing Clinic, Inc. Software author and distributor to audiologists

Using the principles that we've learned at Mr. Sidell's seminars have enriched our lives and changed our course in extremely positive ways. We consider him a mentor, healer and a teacher to the masses...as well as a close friend.

--Dave Buzzalini and Renee Grandieri-Buzzalini, M.S./APN

Over many years and in many fascinating locations it has been my privilege to attend Bob's seminars. They have served as a focal point stimulating my curiosity and my enthusiasm. They have made the future more promising, the present easier to live with.

--Chester M. Sidell, Dermatological Surgeon, and Robert's father

The experience that Robert shares in his seminars and writings is one of wholeness and healing through being in touch with spiritual truth in all of its sweetness and simplicity. Having Robert as a brother I enjoy the opportunity of continuously being reminded of these truths.

--Ivory Sue Sidell, Hair Stylist and Robert's sister

Robert's seminars have been so inpirational to me. They have given proof to me that there really is a Supreme Being that guides our destiny.

--Eleanor Blackburn, Registered Nurse and mother of five, including Robert

I have known Robert Sidell for over 14 years. In my mind he has mastered the beauty of God's love. The principles he teaches are truly uplifting, positive, and spiritually based. One thing I have learned from Robert is to expect miracles and I am never disappointed.
--Susie Hadland, Photographer & Proprietor of Gallery in Sky located in Las Vegas Stratosphere Tower

With Bob's guidance we are shaping our lives into a paradise on earth. We have been blessed beyond measure.
--Misha Zweig, 2nd Grade School Teacher; Jim Sallee, Real Property Department, City of Henderson, 27 years

When I first met Robert I wondered why he always seemed so happy and in a good mood. Then I had an opportunity to speak with him, and he shared a new, more positive way of looking at life. He has shared with me strategies to transform the challenges of every day living into opportunities.
--Dr. Beverly Daly, Principal, Clark County School District

A Rare Opportunity

Your Key to a Miraculous Life

by

Robert B. Sidell

Cate Cummings
Publicity & Promotion Group
7601 East 93rd Street
Kansas City, MO 64138-4206
(816) 767-0396 • Fax (816) 767-0289
Email: Cor@BookPublicity.com
Website: www.BookPublicity.com

A Rare Opportunity
Your Key to a Miraculous Life

Contact Information for Robert Sidell

If you would like more information about books Robert Sidell has written, classes he teaches, or getting on his mailing list, you can contact him toll free at 1-888-384-3847. You may also write him at 3415 West Charleston, Las Vegas, NV 89102, or contact his web page at *www.RobertSidell.com* to send email and find other information about him.

Acknowledgments

I want to thank my wife for her patience in letting me disappear for long times while writing this book. I also want to thank DeLayna Anderson who out of her desire to serve God has worked tirelessly to bring this book into print. I also want to thank all of my spiritual friends who have been the great treasure of my life. Last, and perhaps most importantly, I wish to acknowledge my parents Chester and Eleanor, for all of the love and support they have given me in this life.

DEDICATION

This book is dedicated to all of the great souls who have walked this earth and have made the path through this world easier for each of us today.

May you find what you seek and discover the happiness of a life well lived!

Table of Contents

Forward

Awaken to a Miraculous Life

There is a high road in this life. A road that when traveled will awaken you to a life of joy, peace and prosperity greater than your most wonderful dreams. You can live free from the limitations that shackle so many people, living each day as a wonderful adventure. Every experience can become rich, powerful and filled with joy.

For thousands of years the human race has evolved its technology, learning how to do more and more complicated things in less time. We travel faster, we communicate over great distances, we build great machines and buildings. We have cures for many diseases.

But have people become happier? Have people learned to relax and enjoy life? Has the technology freed people or enslaved them? For most people life has simply become faster, more competitive, and more stressful than ever before. Somehow, most people have failed to truly reap the benefits of our great advances. They move on an ever faster treadmill and don't know how to get off.

Yet it doesn't have to be this way. You can take a great step forward, and literally transform every aspect of your life. **You can live an outrageously prosperous, happy life.** This happiness can continue growing for the rest of your life. You can expand your time, multiply your prosperity, and magnify your opportunities. These are bold, powerful words. But are they true? Can they apply to you, to the facts of your life? **The answer is yes, without a doubt.**

This book is your invitation to awaken to a wonderful new reality. This book will open up vast new vistas of opportunity for you. It will reveal new ways of approaching virtually every circumstance in your life. It will enrich your life spiritually, emotionally and materially. The results will begin immediately, and will continue to grow as you put into practice the ideas presented here.

You will find the obstacles of your life begin to melt away. As they do you will begin to discover your real purpose in life. You will begin to feel a deep inner joy that you always sensed was possible. It will be like awakening from a dream to a reality that you always knew existed. Your life will take on a sense of purpose, vitality and vigor.

This is your opportunity to choose the high road. You will know the truth of this by the inner feeling you get as you read these words. Dare to trust your own inner convictions. This is the beginning of a wonderful adventure for you. Follow the step by step instructions of the book, and be willing to suspend your old attitudes to try out the new ideas presented here. You have nothing to lose and everything to gain!

Introduction

How to Get the Most out of This Book

This book is not like any other book you have read before. Its purpose is to give you a direct experience of the freedom of your soul, and the potentiality you have to live in the world as a free empowered, prosperous being.

In writing this book I have been very careful not to simply throw down words on a piece of paper to make it into a book. I have gone into seclusion at a private retreat and meditated for days until I came into a state of oneness with an incredible experience of joy.

Then, when writing, I have asked for God's will–and only God's will–to be expressed on these pages. I have actually found my hands vibrating with the electricity of divine grace as I have written. In fact, it has been an amazing experience of empowerment for me, probably at least as great as what you will receive.

So, if you feel the connection, I offer you the empowerment that this book has offered to me. Let it be a wind in your sail, a gentle lift up the stairway to your spiritual awakening! May it remove the obstacles in your path and lift you to a future better than you ever imagined!

As you read this book and do the exercises, you will notice a shift in your state of mind. You will notice that you begin to feel more *optimistic* about everything in your life. You will discover a deep sense of *inner calm*. You will feel a sense of your own *power*.

This book is designed to create a direct link with your infinite consciousness. It is actually the creation of your own awareness, a life raft that will carry you to a better quality life. The only real keys for you are these: be open, be receptive, give the ideas a try, and observe your life carefully to notice the transformations that begin to come.

In short, this book can be viewed as a transformational book which has as its purpose the *empowerment of your life, the exaltation of your experience.* Be willing to open yourself to the thought, the idea, the possibility that this is exactly what will happen to you– no matter how far fetched it may seem at this moment. Out of this joy and peace a new future will be born for you: a future with new opportunities, relationships, jobs, spiritual awareness–whatever is right for your life.

If you are ready and willing to have great success and inner peace, these can be available to you immediately. You do not have to have any special background. For all people are endowed with the potential for great success, for the potential of great peace.

Be willing to keep this book with you, and frequently re-read parts that you find inspiring or uplifting. Each time you connect with the book it will act as a lifting, empowering agent in your life. Take the book with you so that while you are relaxing at work you might read a few paragraphs or points in it, and keep rereading whatever sections cause you to realize that you are an unlimited, empowered being.

Above all, have fun!

Chapter 1

Welcome to a Miraculous World

You are a powerful being. Imagine that you are so powerful that you created this book as a tool to rise to an entirely new level of existence. This is, in fact, the truth. You are endowed with the power to dream, to create, and to weave the fabric of your own destiny. You have drawn this book into your life *to empower, to uplift, and to serve as a tool to attain your dreams in life!*

Your primary objective in reading this book is to transform your own experience of life. It is your job, if you so desire, to rebuild your self-experience from the bottom up. No longer will you feel small, inconsequential, and without purpose in a chaotic world. Instead, you will surge with power, peace and happiness because you will have spread your wings and started to fly.

There is no happiness in this world that compares with the experience of awakening to the truth about your own nature. Just as an eagle must learn to fly to fulfill its destiny, so you must learn to use the vast power that has been given to you. It is your destiny and your purpose on this earth.

Commit to opening yourself to the message contained within this book. Commit to awakening to your true inner nature. As you do this, miracles will begin to unfold immediately in every part of your life.

Things are Not as They Appear

This world is not as it appears to be! This realization is the first step on the high road of life. This simple truth has been stated for thousands of years by the great thinkers and teachers. Virtually every major religion teaches that this world is a place without limits, and beyond our ordinary comprehension.

In Christianity it is said that we must learn to live "in" the world, but not be "of" it. It is said that faith is the evidence of things unseen, the substance of things hoped for. In the Hindu tradition it is said that Maya causes us to see this world through the eyes of delusion, not really recognizing our true nature, or the nature of the world.

Simply put, this world is a magical place: A place where all things are possible for the person that awakens to his or her fullest potential. *This cannot be proven to you.* It is something that you can only discover by looking to your own inner experience.

In this way life is completely fair. We must all take that great step into the unknown, the unprovable part of this reality. Only when we are willing to transcend, to reach beyond everything our rational mind would tell us, are we ready to step forward into the enlightened, illumined life. Only at that point can we begin to wield the great power that is ours to use.

The high road is not a path for one who does not have courage. It takes great courage to face the appearance of negativity, scarcity, limitation, and to proclaim and transform those appearances into abundance, peace, happiness and freedom. Yet this is precisely the opportunity that is available to us during our sojourn here on this planet. To remember that which is beyond the memory; to become that which is not possible. For the impossible to *become* possible.

Why not make your life something worthwhile, something great? Why not reach for the stars? You might discover that you *are* the stars!

Each story, each idea you will read in this book is based on what I have learned through my own experience, or observed from other people's experiences. These experiences prove beyond a shadow of a doubt that there are unlimited possibilities in this world. Just like you, I have made many mistakes. I am not embarrassed to admit that in this world that we learn through mistakes; I wasn't born walking –were you?

Set aside you ego, your certainty that you understand exactly how this life works. Open yourself to the truth that resides in your own soul. Let that experience fill you now, a sense of the vast possibilities that are waiting for you right now. Let yourself feel how happy God is for you to finally say, "I am ready to awaken, to assume my destiny!" What a wonderful adventure you will then embark upon. What joy awaits you, what peace, what happiness!

You are a Miracle Worker

In this unlimited world we are each miracle workers, creating with our thoughts, words and deeds. From moment to moment we are creating our destiny through the dominant thoughts we hold, the words we speak, the actions we follow them with.

Unfortunately, I did not learn this the easy way. Like so many people, I was wielding this great power very carelessly and ignorantly. In truth, I didn't realize what power I had.

For this is the great deception, the great illusion of life. It appears that the world is constantly happening to us, and that we are just bystanders to this spectacle. We do not see how we are planting the seeds at every moment that will turn up as the circumstances of our life tomorrow!

I created My Own Failure!

I have known both great success and great failure in my life. In law school I was riding high. In my second semester of law school I was number one in a class of over 200 students. I went on to graduate from one of the top law schools in the country in the top 10% of my class. Later I took a job at an internationally renowned law firm that had many major clients, including President Reagan.

Yet, sometime after I got out of law school I began to have a crisis in confidence. I started seeing the world and my life personally from a negative point of view. I started making comments to those closest to me about the negative prospects for my future.

The work at the law firm was highly competitive, and I really didn't enjoy what I was doing. The real estate market was soaring and it seemed like a house would always be out of reach. It was very easy to feel sorry for myself (that is never very hard, is it!). I started thinking that things had been much easier even a few years earlier, when the costs were down in the real estate market, and the legal market was less competitive.

I started saying things like "I'll never be able to own a home," and "I can't see any future in this work where I will be happy." I didn't view my marriage through positive eyes, but instead began to think about its deficiencies. Unfortunately, as you know, these types of patterns are easy to fall into.

I thought and spoke negatively about most of the major things in my life. Of course, at the time I simply thought it was being "realistic." *That was my critical error.* You see, at that time in my life I believed that the world "happened" to me.

I didn't think my thoughts or spoken words had any great impact on the actual conditions and circumstances in my life. Like so many people I blindly went about creating the destruction of much of what I loved.

In a matter of only a few short years I brought a good marriage to an end, and practically destroyed my career. I was so broke that I had to borrow money from a friend to buy a jar of peanut butter.

From where I was standing it looked like success was coming easily to everyone else, and I was missing some key point (which, in fact I was). I started wondering whether life wasn't some sort of cruel hoax, dangling all sorts of wonderful possibilities in front of you, only to withdraw them at the last moment. I was bankrupt, and jobless, with little prospects for the future. I came to the point where I really didn't want to continue living. Fortunately, I never acted upon that desire.

There can be a tremendous fatigue and despair that sets in when you start to believe you can never be free, never successful. Almost every human being faces this feeling at some point in their life. That is why I am writing this book– to help you find the great success to which you are entitled – so you can avoid my mistakes.

But there is a *silver lining* to such despair. It is out of such a depth of feeling that the soul can make a tremendous leap forward. When you can see no way out, no light at the end of the tunnel, you are faced with two choices: either give up and die, or do the impossible–become something greater than you have ever been.

It is just this depth of desire that releases enormous transforming power within the human soul. It is this type of desire that heals cancer and other irreversible health conditions. It is the power that resides at the core of the human soul. When we cry out from the depth of our soul for help, Life will respond. An answer will be sent. This is the great miracle of creation.

For those of us that are hard headed (usually the greater the success, the more agreement a person has had in life, the more hardheaded they are), it may take this type of fall for us to begin to look inward. Something within us begins to say there must be a better way, there must be a new possibility of life. With this crack in the cosmic egg of our consciousness, suddenly the inflow of great wisdom can begin.

The Answer Came To Me

The great revelation for me came when I started closely examining the pattern of my own life. I saw that at one point in my life I had been very positive about my future. At that time I did extraordinarily well, but when I started thinking and speaking negatively I surely began to reap negative outcomes. I know you may be thinking this is overly simplistic, but most truly profound insights are simple.

I discovered that the world we live in is a boundless, unlimited field of energy in which we are free to create our destinies according to our own thoughts, words and actions. We, are, in fact creating our destinies whether we realize it or not.

Suddenly, as if in a brilliantly lit movie, I looked back over my life and saw that there was always an inexorable connection between what I thought, what I said, and what happened. In case after case I saw how my circumstances had first *originated in my own mind,* through worry, doubt, and conversations with the people around me. What would begin as worries or repeated thoughts, would invariably show up in my life as actual circumstances. Sometimes the outcomes were almost comical as I looked back.

For example, I was looking for a house. My wife and I dearly wanted one, as many young couples do. But as the prices seemed to soar I began to get resentful, and frequently stated to her "we will never find a house, we will never own a house." One time we actually found what seemed to be the perfect house. It was a beautiful home, in our price range, had been on the market for over six months.

"we will never find a house, we will never own a house." One time we actually found what seemed to be the perfect house. It was a beautiful home, in our price range, had been on the market for over six months.

We only wanted to offer $5,000 less than the owner was asking for. We asked our realtor to give the offer to the owner right then while we were in the house. We were confident he would accept and we would get the house. The realtor asked if she could delay for a few hours because she had an open house to attend. We agreed–after all what would a few hours delay be after six months on the market? Three hours later we received a call from our realtor. The house had been sold to someone else for *less* than we had been willing to pay. A buyer had come along, and made the offer in that 3-hour interval.

At the time we lost this house, it was to me, just one more example of the unfairness of life, of the generally difficult conditions I was facing. It just became one more justification for developing a negative attitude about things. I proceeded to tell everyone about how we had lost this house, and how unfair it seemed. But later, as I looked back on this incident I began to realize that I had planted the seeds of this failure. By constantly repeating, over and over again, that I would never own a house, I was literally creating that destiny. I had directed my subconscious to make sure I wouldn't own a house!

Of course this was just one of many circumstances in my life that appeared to be connected to my own thinking, my own response to life. I could give you examples from my work, from my marriage, from every part of my life.

Notice carefully your response to this story. Are you thinking that it really couldn't be this way–that our thoughts and remarks create outcomes–even negative outcomes? If that is your response you are no different than I was at that time. All I can say to you is consider the possibility that we really *do* create our destiny through our words and thoughts.

Could it be this simple, is it possible that we do have such great power?

Use Your Spoken Words Like a Magic Wand – To Create What You Want

I immediately set out to test my idea that our lives originate in our minds. I began to use my spoken word like a "magic wand." Simply put, I talked about my life the way I wanted it to be, *not the way it appeared at the time!* I spoke, thought, and acted positively about my life, about opportunity, about the world, and about the future. After all, I was at the bottom in my own life, so I had nothing to lose.

I knew I needed a new beginning in my life so I moved to a new town where I didn't know even one person. I took a job with the District Attorney's office. I had no savings, no reserves. I borrowed my first month rent from my ex-wife.

Shortly after I arrived in my new town, the voters decided to "rollback the property tax." This created a budget crunch and led to the layoff of 200 people from the District Attorney's office, including me. There I was in a new town, knowing very few people, without a job, and no savings to speak of. *What would you do under such circumstances?*

Layoff Led to New Business Started With No Capital

When the layoff occurred I knew that this was the time to "put up or shut up" – it was time for me to create a positive, successful future by keeping my mind focused on good, through speaking positively, and refusing to succumb to pessimism. The events that followed proved to me beyond a shadow of a doubt that *we live in a magical, empowered world.*

When I first heard the news of my layoff I was worried. Where would I work? What would I do? I discovered that talking and acting in a positive way is one thing, but *living it is more difficult!* But then I began to see that a wonderful opportunity was available to me.

I could proceed in faith, trusting and knowing that only good would come to me. I could trust completely in the power greater than myself to guide me every step of the way to my highest good! *I knew that if I could succeed in "creating" my way out of this situation I would be free for the rest of my life.*

First, I consciously avoided any tendency to feel anger, upset or fear. I made a creativity board (see Chapter 6) on which I placed pictures and slogans representing the lifestyle I wanted. I wrote out the qualities I desired to have in a job. *The miracles starting manifesting immediately!*

Within 30 minutes of the time that the actual layoff notice was given I received a call from a man that I had only met once, telling me of a possible job. The job was guaranteed for only a month but would give me time to look for a permanent job. I was laid off the last Friday in August and started on the new job on the next Monday.

Then the unexpected occurred (as it often does when you open yourself to the miracle working power of this universe). The law firm that had hired me for the one-month position suddenly split up. One partner left, with the result that office space became available. When the end of my one-month job approached the remaining attorney made an offer I could not refuse: *free office space if I wanted it, until I could get enough clients of my own to begin paying rent.*

Try to imagine the probability of this occurring! Free office space in an expensive office building offered to me until I began to make a profit–needless to say, I accepted the offer.

The miracles continued. One of the members of my church called and referred to me an excellent case. I was able to settle it within two months (which is almost unheard of) and earn an $8,000 fee.

This was the seed money that allowed me to begin paying rent at my office and start my own private practice. Again, try to imagine the probability of receiving such a case, one that would pay off so soon. Many attorneys never get such a case in their entire career.

Suddenly, my practice was mushrooming! I had so much work by the end of that year, I hired an excellent attorney as my assistant. Within 1 ½ years I had one attorney, three secretaries, and a receptionist all employed by my office! *All in a town where I hadn't known a single person less than a year earlier!*

In the following year I earned more than the top salary available at the office I had been laid off from, with much greater freedom and control in my life. Later I had the chance to purchase an office building for $100,000 below its appraised value, with almost no money down.

Many years have passed since that time. The journey has not always been smooth. There have been challenges of every kind that occur in business. Yet through faith the path has always been upward, the success greater, the freedom more complete.

My layoff experience taught me a profound and valuable lesson about life: no matter what our circumstances, no matter what has happened, if we are willing to master our thought, to use our word as a magic wand, and to proceed with positive follow up, we can go on to great success!

You can do this in your life as well. No matter what has happened in your life, whether on a business or personal level–divorce, bankruptcy, it doesn't matter. You can begin again and go on to accomplish great things. Even if you are already successful, you can grow in your success, and deepen your happiness by learning to master your spoken word, your thinking and your actions. *This is the magic kingdom, and you must simply remember that to be free!*

University Professor Proves that Words Carry Power

Imagine my excitement when I found Martin Seligman's book, *Learned Optimism (Alfred A. Knopf, Publisher, NY.1991)* which made a multi generational study of people's speech and thinking patterns, and the effect it had on their lives. Martin E. P. Seligman, PHD, is UPS Foundation Professor of Social Science and Director of Clinical Training in Psychology at the University of Pennsylvania.

He found in case after case that you could tell how successful a person would be based on his or her speaking and thinking style! People that were optimistic consistently were healthier, lived longer, and less likely to get depressed. This applied not only to individuals, but also to entire groups of people such as sports teams or families. In his book he stated:

"These two habits of thinking about causes have consequences. Literally hundreds of studies show that pessimists give up more easily and get depressed more often. These experiments also show that optimists do much better in school and college, at work and on the playing field. They regularly exceed predictions of aptitude tests. When optimists run for office they are more apt to be elected than pessimists are. Their health is unusually good. They age well, much freer than most of us from the usual physical ills of middle age. Evidence suggests they may even live longer."

For those with doubting minds, this provides very strong evidence that the way we think and speak has a very profound and important effect on our lives.

Ignorance of the Law is No Defense

In law there is a rule: "Ignorance of the law is no defense." This rule was adopted to prevent people engaged in criminal behavior from later claiming they didn't know what the law was. It is much the same with "universal law."

Even if we are ignorant of the effects of gravity we still experience its effects. Try going to a balcony some day and walking off. *You will fall whether you know about gravity or not!* Water will boil at 212 degrees whether you know it or not.

In the same way, we are all subject to the laws of creation whether we understand them or not. A person who innocently thinks and speaks negatively will surely reap negative results whether or not he or she is aware of it. This is why some people so consistently create the same kinds of dramas in their own lives over and over again. We have all seen it – and all done it ourselves!

This is why it is so important to become aware of these laws of creation, and begin to use them constructively to produce great happiness. The choice is yours. *Why don't you start today, thinking, speaking, and acting more positively than you ever have before! You will awaken to a future more wonderful than you ever imagined!*

Victim or Master, the Choice is Yours

It can be very confronting to the ego and to the mind to face the fact that we have created much unnecessary suffering in our lives. For this reason there is a very critical stage on the path to the high road to awakened living. When we begin to see the role we have played in our own creation of life we are presented with two possibilities: one leads to freedom, the other leads to continued suffering.

You see, precisely because it can be painful to see what we have created, it may seem more pleasant to continue seeing yourself as a victim of circumstances beyond your control. At least then you don't have to consider whether the suffering you went through was self-generated and unnecessary, which can be quite a blow.

If you choose to see yourself as a victim in a world that spins out of control (which is the mainstream viewpoint of reality), you will certainly have much support. You can find all kinds of friends to support you in that belief, and probably give you a lot of sympathy as well. But what kind of life will you be creating and living? A life with a lot of problems, a lot of suffering, and a lot of sympathy. *I don't know about you, but that isn't the kind of life I want!*

On the other hand, you can breathe deeply, face your own life, and begin to honestly assess the role you have played in its creation until now. You can carefully examine your thinking, your actions, and your habits and begin to see how they have woven the destiny that you are currently living. This may be very confronting on some level, mostly because you will see just how unnecessary much of your suffering has been.

But if you persist, if you are willing to bare your soul, and totally open yourself to the truth, something wonderful will happen. You will experience a healing of your past, and you will be on the high road to living a life more joyous than you could possibly imagine.

Let me tell you a *simple story* that will always stick in your memory to illustrate the choice we must all make:

Imagine that two people have been given beautiful cars to drive. The road they must drive sometimes has some sharp bends, and a lot of traffic. It requires careful driving. It can be quite scary to make the journey.

The first driver starts to become scared about the possibility of an accident, so he decides to close his eyes. He figures at least he won't have to be afraid. Well, you can imagine that he begins to get in one accident after the other. Pretty soon he decides he will never open his eyes because all that is going to happen is that he will see an accident coming. He figures that although his car is getting all banged up, and he is getting pretty bruised up at least he doesn't have to see the accident coming. He never makes it to the end of the journey. His car gets destroyed, and he is in very poor health from all of the accidents. But he does get a lot of sympathy from his friends about the terrible road conditions in today's world.

The other driver realizes that there are risks, but would rather keep his eyes open. At times that makes him scared, but he usually is able to take evasive action and avoid accidents. Pretty soon he is able to drive much faster, and pull free from other risks. He gets to his destination free from damage, and in wonderful health. He has time to enjoy, and is very happy.

Which driver would you rather be? If you want to keep your eyes open, this book is for you! *Victim or master, the choice is yours.*

Choose today to master your life and realize your fullest potential. You will accomplish great things!

Summary and Action Plan

1. This World is a Magical Place where all things are possible!

2. You are continually creating your reality from moment to moment with your dominant thoughts, words and deeds.

3. You can change your life if you are willing to change your thoughts, words and deeds.

4. Proof exists that people who speak positively live happier, healthier, longer, more successful lives. You can do it too!

Exercise:

A. Start today to use your word as a magic wand, speaking about your life the way you want it to be. Be bold, and imaginative. Speak in glorious terms about your life– after all your life is a magnificent creation.

B. For 30 days closely monitor your thoughts and words, and if you notice a negative thought replace it with a positive one! Refuse to say or think negative things about anything! See what happens. At the end of 30 days, if you like the results, start over for another 30 days!

C. Observe the connection between your thoughts and the circumstances in your life. Practice listening to other people's conversations and notice what happens in their lives.

D. No matter where you are in your life, or what exists right now, you can create a wonderful future, and create limitless opportunity. It is never too late!

Chapter 2

Are you Living Your Dream?

Deep within we all know that we can a live a life that is higher, more glorious, and more meaningful than we are living. We inwardly know that we are destined for greatness– greatness of joy, prosperity, and peace. Something continues to lift us to new aspirations, new dreams, and new goals.

Dare to dream bold, imaginative, powerful dreams, for in your dreams lies your salvation. In your dreams lies your very destiny. Your dreams will keep you young. Your dreams will give you energy. Your dreams will give you good health. Your dreams will keep you alive, and give you a life better than you ever imagined.

Don't be afraid to reach for the stars. As you reach, so you will be created. God dreams of the person great enough to dream of God, the person who is not afraid to ask for it all, to create it all, to dare to be fully awakened.

You can and *will* accomplish great things in this life, if you will just open yourself to your higher self, and be willing to follow the inner guidance you receive.

Give Yourself a Checkup

The test for each of us is whether we are moving in the direction of our dreams. We must be willing to be completely honest about where we are and how we have been living our lives until now. We can never move ahead without being honest about where we are!

Take a few minutes in a private setting and answer the following questions:

Are you living your own dream?

Take some time and think carefully about this question. Are you living your life according to the dictates of others? Are you simply doing what you "should" be doing, but not really what excites you?

Far too many of us allow our dreams to die a slow death, pretending that we never had them. Look honestly. Are you living the life *you* want to live? If not, why not? We each have the ability to move steadily in the direction of our dreams.

Do you look forward to each day?

Do you wake up with anticipation of the opportunities to be alive in this wonderful world? You can learn to view each day with great excitement, like a child would anticipate Christmas or a birthday. You have the ability to create your life so you sleep in peace, and wake up in joy! If this is not the way your life is, then you should open yourself to change.

Are you filled with energy, vitality and enthusiasm for your life?

This life is a wondrous opportunity. Every day we can learn to live in greater joy, peace, and happiness. As we move towards our dreams we become filled with vitality and energy. If you don't feel this way it is probably a sign that you need to re-evaluate the way you are living, and what you are doing.

Do you view your work as play?

If your work is simply drudgery, you need to change what you do! There is no reason to spend a huge amount of your life engaging in activities you don't enjoy. You have the capability to support yourself in ways that you enjoy and give you tremendous rewards (see Chapter 10 on How to Master your Work).

Are you doing what you do best?

You have certain special gifts, things that you do wonderfully, and effortlessly. These are the things that you should be doing on a daily basis. You will contribute most to the people around you by doing so.

When you finish answering the preceding questions you should have a very good sense of how you are doing so far in your life. There is no reason why you cannot set up your life to say yes to each of the foregoing questions. The next section will give you a chance to look at what *you really want for your life.* It is only by learning what you want that you will find the happiness you seek.

Chart Your Dreams

Strangely enough, the major problem most people have in their lives is deciding what they want! It is so easy to let society influence our choices, our decisions about virtually everything. Instead of thinking, conscious human beings we become like robots living out someone else's projections of how life should be.

Imagine life as a river with a strong current. The culture we are born into is the river we have been immersed in. Unless we make a strong decision to honor our own feelings, perceptions and values, the current will govern our lives.

If we aren't careful, we will be swept along, having few original thoughts or dreams. Doing life just like everyone else. Never really tasting the supreme joy that is available. *But there is a better way!* We can stop, get out of the rut and start thinking for ourselves. Take the time to follow through with this chapter, with this book, and your life really will *exceed your most wonderful dreams.*

You have already given yourself a "checkup" in the preceding section, and have a sense of how you are doing. The purpose of this section is to get you thinking about what you do want, what your dreams *really* are. In order to get the most out of this section, be willing to let your mind *soar! Give up being realistic for a while–you have spent most of your life being realistic.* As you go through these questions, write down whatever comes to your mind no matter how improbable or unrealistic it seems to you. For each question, focus on your *spiritual, emotional, physical, relationship and material* dreams.

If you had only six months to live, what would you do with your time?

We all have a tendency to defer or put off the things that are important in our lives. We procrastinate and assume we will get to them when we have more time. The truth is that unless we start today on our dreams we will probably never attain them. Think carefully about this question, and consider your answers in each of the following areas:

(1) *Spiritual.* What spiritual changes would you make? Would you attempt to find a deeper relationship to God? What would you do differently? It has been said, a wise man makes time for God, because it is God that makes all time for man. There are so many ways to accomplish this, but it is undoubtedly your most important job in this life! See Chapter 14 for further discussion of developing your divine connection in life.

(2) *Emotional.* What emotional changes do you want? Would you like to experience greater inner peace, joy and happiness–less anger and jealousy? List whatever comes to mind. Remember *you* are in charge of your mind. You can choose how you are going to use it, and learn to find great happiness.

(3) *Physical.* What health changes do you want? Do you want to feel radiantly healthy and filled with endless energy? Do you want to grow younger, and more vibrant as time passes? Would you change your diet? Do you want to exercise more, and

bring your body into better condition? Remember that your health has an incredible impact on your daily experience of life.

(4) *Relationships.* What relationship changes would you make? Would you contact people to resolve incomplete communications? Would you seek to develop new relationships, or perhaps commit more deeply to your current relationship? Are there new people you would like to reach out to in your life? Are there people you want to release? Would you like to spend more time with your family?

(5) *Material.* How would you like to be earning your living? What level of income do you want? What possessions would you acquire? What would you let go of? Many times we end up accumulating things that we have no use for. Could you release possessions and make your life more enjoyable? Would you like to travel to new places, do new things? Would you like to have more time, or make better use of your time?

If you could work miracles, what would you create?

We are so used to being "realistic" about our dreams, that we often have forgotten how to let our imaginations soar. Do you remember the dreams and fantasies you had as a child? You didn't worry about what other people thought, or whether the dreams were realistic. Your mind knew no limits, and you were highly creative. But somewhere on the path to growing up you learned to be "realistic," to place limits on your mind.

When answering this question, have fun! Try to think of what you would do, in your personal life and in the world if you had the miraculous power to create things exactly the way you wanted to. Go through the same list of categories and write out your goals without any concern about the probability of success.

You will find it is great fun to let your imagination go wild. Would you create multiple houses? Would you have phenomenal health? Would you set up your life to have as much time as you want to pursue the activities of your choice? What kind of relationships would you create if there were no limit on your power to create? What would you do in the world? Would you bring peace to the world? Would you feed the poor? What would you choose to do with your miraculous power? How would the world look when you were done?

This exercise can produce amazing results in your life. You may find that a dream that you thought was totally remote–and unlikely–will appear much sooner than you ever imagined. Most importantly, it will begin to resurrect your power to dream, to think creatively. Remember that there is always an idea to solve every problem because the human mind is an unlimited idea generator!

Jaguar Obtained!

I experimented with this process in my own life to obtain a Jaguar automobile. At one time, approximately 10 years ago, I had the fantasy of having a Jaguar. Somehow, the idea of owning that kind of car was very exciting to me. So when I wrote my written goals for the year, I put down that I wanted a Jaguar.

When I wrote it down I was very aware that it was low on my priority list, and probably wouldn't come into my life (or so I thought). About a month after I had written the goal, I was having dinner with a good friend in a Japanese restaurant.

As we were leaving he introduced me to an older gentleman, who casually mentioned that he had two Jaguars in his garage. I asked if he had ever considered selling the cars. He said that he had been thinking about it but wanted to find a good owner for it, who would finish the restoration.

I took the bait, and went to the see the cars. As you can probably guess, I had to have one. I became extraordinarily excited. Within two weeks the car was mine, which was the beginning of a long adventure with many different chapters. But the important point is that I had listed what seemed to me to be an outrageous goal, and yet it had come into reality almost instantly.

We must always remain open to having our goals fulfilled much quicker than we think. There is no time in the universe, and there is no order of difficulty in miracles. *If we are ready, and if the time is right, things can happen almost instantly!*

Make a decision to sit down and write down your goals at least once a year if not more often. Put down every conceivable dream, from the ordinary to the extraordinary. Let God decide which ones are right for you!

Stand Up for Your Dreams

He Sailed Around the World!

A friend of mine had a dream to sail around the world. Bill was about 45 years old and worked for a major manufacturing company. He was successful, and his position was secure. Yet he had a persistent dream that he wanted to get out and see the world. He talked it over with his wife and family. At first his wife wasn't thrilled by the thought, but gradually she came to like the idea.

But he found that his parents were very threatened by his desire to leave his secure job and begin sailing. His father even threatened to disinherit him if he left his job. This troubled Bill since his father was not in good health and he didn't want to upset him.

Yet in his heart he felt certain that this was the right thing for him to do. So he and his wife started making plans to begin this journey. They sold their house and bought a large yacht. They moved into the yacht so they could save as much money as possible. Their planning went on for three years.

Eventually the day came when it was time to go. Bill went to meet with his father. Amazingly, his opposition had been transformed. Over the three years of preparation his father had come to realize how much it meant to him. He even offered to help out in whatever way he could.

I met Bill in Costa Rica when he had been traveling for over 11 months, going from one country to the next. I will always remember what he told me. He was having the best time of his life. He was having so much fun he said he had to "pinch" himself to see if it was really happening.

Both he and his wife had come to know each other much better, they had grown closer to their own family, and even had the support of his father. Believe it or not, their trip will take them five years. They have planned it out, and are right on schedule. He was living his dream, and you can too!

Bill's story illustrates what so often is true. We must be willing to stand up for our dreams. Sometimes it is the people closest to us that will provide the most resistance. Yet, when we peacefully persist, we may be surprised to discover these very people become our staunchest supporters.

Take the First Step!

It has been said that the journey of a thousand miles begins with a single step. This was literally true for Diane, a wonderful young lady who took one of my seminars. She had always dreamed of living in the Virgin Islands. But for some reason, she had deferred her dream, thinking it unrealistic.

A trip to the Virgin Islands

Diane had the usual doubts. How would she make it? What would her child do? What about her work and current relationships? Diane finally decided that she had nothing to lose and everything to gain. She committed to move to the Virgin Islands. She set a date and time frame.

Once she made that commitment a series of wonderful events commenced. First, she got laid off from her job. You might be thinking what is so wonderful about getting laid off? But for her it gave the necessary freedom she needed to move. So she decided to take a vacation in the Virgin Islands and check out her destination.

When she returned she had great news. She had found a place to live, and a job. On that particular island getting a place to live was no small accomplishment; apartments were very hard to come by, yet she had found hers on the first day she was there. She also received a job offer at a hotel before her trip had ended. In the span of her short vacation she had removed the final obstacles to moving.

She has proceeded with the move and has now been down there for almost two years. She loves being on the small peaceful island, surrounded by the abundant greenery. She writes to me and tells me how much she is enjoying her life.

None of this would have happened if she had not dared to take the first step. *You can do the same thing in your life. What dream have you been putting off? Are you willing to get started today?*

Trust the Ideas that Come to You, They are Gifts to You!

How many times have you had an idea, never acted upon it, only to see someone else turn it into a profitable venture? It certainly has happened to me, and to most people. Why does this happen?

Too often, when we get an idea, somehow we can't really believe it could be that great. We subconsciously assume that if we thought of it, it must be an ordinary idea, not worthy of further pursuit.

Nurse Starts Own Business

Ellen, another friend who took one of my seminars several years ago was a nurse who had always dreamed of starting her own management business. She had a business idea, which she felt would be valuable to hospitals. So many of us have ideas such as these but never act on them. Somehow we just don't believe we will be successful. But Ellen decided to proceed, and started her business. The success she attained was amazing. Soon she had several hospitals as clients, and a number of employees. Then she branched out to multiple states. Her income soared. She was able to buy a beautiful home, and travel extensively. She took safaris in Africa, and lived a highly creative life. Her business provided jobs for many people.

None of this would have been possible if she just kept that idea inside of her head instead of pursuing it. *What idea do you have that you could start pursuing? Why not start today?*

The only way you will ever become the person you want to be is to try out your ideas. Some will fail, but some will succeed. Millionaires are those who have failed most! Unless you are willing to fail, you can never hope to truly attain success in this life! Honor the ideas that come to you.

Watch out for the Thought Police!

The greatest test you will ever face will come when you begin to move in the direction of your dreams. The test will come in the form of your own inner doubts, and the doubts expressed by your friends. All of a sudden, that wonderful idea you had will seem suspect at best. You will wonder why you were ever so foolish to have dreamed you could do it.

The thought police are all those well-meaning people (including your own mind, in many cases) that will try to talk you out of pursuing your dream. They have many reasons for doing this.

In some cases it is threatening to them that you would consider following your dream. After all, they gave up their dreams, why shouldn't you? When they see you moving out to reclaim your life, it reminds them of their own failure to do so.

It is easier for them to discourage you than to face their own lives. In other cases, people are just genuinely concerned for you. This is the most difficult to deal with since you will be inclined to listen and believe.

This is where having a group of supportive friends, or even just one other person (such as a husband or wife) that believes in you can make all the difference.

Summary and Action Plan

1. Your dreams hold great power to transform your life. They contain energy, vibrancy and power. Dare to follow them!

2. Your dreams will rapidly start coming into your life –effortlessly–once you begin to act on this process. Why? Because you are a being of great power, and you draw to yourself everything necessary to accomplish your dreams. Dare to believe, and your success will be greater than you ever imagined.

Exercise:

A. Write out your dreams in the categories listed in the dream process. Be willing to free associate. Don't restrict the activity of your mind. Just relax and pay attention to what you feel. Write them in your book so you will have easy reference to them.

B. After you have listed your spiritual, relationship, material and emotional goals, have fun listing the dreams you would manifest if you could work miracles. Pretend you are a child, and dig deep into your mind. You will find all sorts of dreams that you may have forgotten.

C. Remember –your dreams are waiting for you to discover them! Pursue them and take the first step towards them. Everything else will unfold spontaneously.

Chapter 3

Dare to Prosper!

It is God's good pleasure to give you the kingdom! This message comes in so many ways, in so many different traditions. But the simple fact is that, as you ascend the spiritual path, there is a life of full balanced prosperity waiting for you. Prosperity is so much more than a big bank account. It is a life where your spiritual, financial, emotional and physical needs are met in abundance. It is having a richness of time, good health, and wonderful friends. It is generous living, attempting to help others whenever you can.

If you wish to experience a prosperous life *you must first be sold on the idea that prosperity is good.* Most of us have been programmed with many negative ideas about prosperity. But the simple fact is that your prosperity is good for you and everyone else!

Prosperity is Good for All!

When you live a prosperous life you make a gift to everyone! Prosperity blesses all, and takes from no one. Your prosperity and freedom will increase in this world naturally as you learn to live a balanced spiritual life. When you dare to create great prosperity many people are lifted into prosperity along with you. You serve everyone in your world.

The simple truth is that there is an infinite supply to draw from. As you expand your awareness of what can be brought forth on this earth you simply expand the possibilities for everyone! Every work of art, every beautiful building, every great invention is a form of manifested prosperity. Without prosperity we human beings would still be living in caves, freezing in the winter, and losing three out of five children before adulthood.

When you reach for your dreams you become an inspiration to all who know you. As you reach and manifest dreams, so, too, will they begin to do so. Prosperity begets further prosperity. If you ever want to see poverty, go to nations where they have attempted to wipe out accumulations of wealth: they are usually so successful that everyone lives in poverty!

Put very simply, prosperity is contagious. As you prosper people will catch your state of mind. They will begin to open themselves to living more fully, more creatively in the world. Prosperity is exciting, liberating and beneficial.

As you grow in prosperity, the time will come when you have plenty of money for every good desire and need. *Strangely enough, you will find that you need less money and have more!* You will find that opportunities just seem to pop up in your world. Opportunities to buy things at amazingly low prices, or to earn more money.

It is a strange phenomenon that as we become freer in our lives, our needs actually become reduced. This is because you will no longer spend your time coveting things just to establish your self worth, or to impress others. When you can have anything, and that soaks into your mind, then you no longer will be compulsive about acquiring things.

Overcome Your Limiting Beliefs about Prosperity

If we are serious about living free in this world, we must honestly face the negative ideas that have been given to us regarding prosperity. The Judeo/Christian heritage has many statements that float around in the back of our minds. We have all heard that it is harder for a rich man to get into heaven than a camel through the eye of the needle. These types of thoughts linger in our consciousness and can be a roadblock towards the manifestation of great success.

Yet if we examine spiritual leaders, almost all were very prosperous people. Christ did not live a long life, but clearly he could have whatever he wanted. He could manifest food, wine, or whatever he needed whenever he needed it. If that isn't prosperity, what is? You can see that he had mastered this physical universe. Always keep in mind that Christ taught that we can "do greater things" than he did.

I propose to you that at least one of the purposes of Christ's life was to show us that we can be free, that we can live lives that transcend this physical world. Didn't he teach that God can be our source for all things? This is the essential teaching of all great religions: that we can look to the infinite for all supply, all good, for all time.

Bargain in Life for a Penny and That's All You Will Get

Sometimes good, well-meaning people feel–on some sort of subconscious level– that by staying poor, they are somehow helping others. *Nothing could be further from the truth.* It really is very simple. Our job in life is to constantly free our consciousness to live with greater, more empowered experiences of life. True mastery is complete freedom on every level of human existence. We do no favors to anyone by holding onto small, limited experiences of reality.

Imagine two people going down to the ocean. One takes a teaspoon because that is all he thinks he is entitled to. The other takes all the water he needs, makes salt and benefits everyone. Jobs are created, food is preserved, and good is manifested. The person that took the teaspoon did no favors to anyone; he only limited his own expression of prosperity.

This World Holds Unlimited Potential for Prosperity

With the right idea, there is no limit on beneficial prosperity. No matter what the activity, there is always a way to do it better, a way that serves more people. There are better ways to grow food, to produce clothing, to build housing than have even been thought of today. When those ideas are brought forth, not only will great wealth be generated; the standard of living for all will rise.

There is no reason why we cannot maintain this world beautifully, in harmony with nature, while still growing in prosperity, peace and happiness. However, the real key for living with greater prosperity for all people is the need for human beings to learn to live together in peace!

He Dared to Prosper and Now Employs Thousands in Las Vegas

If you have visited Las Vegas recently you know it is a booming, thriving town. This prosperity is at least in part due to the willingness of Steve Wynn to dream of prosperity and success on a truly grand scale.

When I first moved to Las Vegas 14 years ago, Steve Wynn was the owner of an older casino in the downtown area. This was the less glamorous, older section of Las Vegas.

Shortly after I arrived, he started engaging in a major renovation of the hotel. Soon it was as beautiful as any of the major casinos on the strip. Its success soared. Many people would have stopped there, having created a very successful business.

But Steve Wynn decided he wanted to build a resort on the famous Las Vegas Strip. He wanted to build the best resort in Las Vegas. Of course the strip was lined with huge, successful casinos already. This didn't stop him. He went ahead and designed the Mirage Hotel and Casino. This hotel was such a vast complex, and required so much funding to build, *that it was reported to require revenues of a million dollars a day just to break even!*

Stop and reflect a moment! Would you have had the courage to dare to create a business that had an overhead of a million dollars a day? What if it flopped? What if people didn't like the resort? All of your success would evaporate.

In spite of these concerns, the dream of the Mirage hotel became a reality. Today it is one of the most beautiful hotels in Las Vegas. You can watch a huge volcano erupting every 30 minutes. You can see dolphins swimming where there was once only desert.

This kind of possibility thinking has tremendous positive spin off effects. The Mirage and its various businesses directly employ thousands of people. Thousands of additional people have jobs providing the services to all of those people.

Most of the other major casinos also decided to upgrade, inspired at least in part by the success of the Mirage. So now the Las Vegas Casinos are among the most modern, elegant and exciting in the world. Las Vegas is one of the most successful cities in the world.

Success breeds success. It is contagious. Allow people to prosper, and there is no limit to the growth that can occur. By the way, Steve Wynn has now built his newest venture. It is to be the "best" hotel, to be built on the old site of the Dunes hotel. It is the Bellagio, and has recently opened to great fanfare. Again, the gamble was taken, the gamble on excellence.

What dreams do you have? Can you start today? Can you see that your dreams benefit everyone?

Housewife Prospers and Everyone Benefits

You may have a simpler dream that beckons you forward. A friend of mine who was a housewife, became excited by a dream of working with businesses to empower and inspire them. This could have just remained in her mind, and she could have never taken any action. Instead she proceeded to receive training on how to inspire and educate people. She then began actively marketing her program. Today she has a successful motivational seminar company. She has offices in multiple states and employs many people. She has a beautiful yacht that she spends her weekends on, and a retreat in the country where she teaches her courses.

She is now grossing over $3,000,000 per year, maintains a home in Mexico and the United States. She recently said to me that all she had was a dream a little over 10 years ago. She started with no money, nothing but an idea! I asked her what she attributed her success to. She told me that she had a vision and held it in her mind until it turned into reality. She also added that one must follow a vision with action to create results!

All of these things came to pass because she was willing to dream, and follow up her dream with action. As she prospered many others prospered as well. Wouldn't it be sad if she had feared prosperity, feared success, and failed to start her business? Think of all the people that work for her that would be worse off, not to mention those whom she educates.

This one prosperous life has lifted many others to prosperity. You, too, can lift others to prosperity if you are willing to follow your inner prompting. You have the seeds of greatness within you. Let them sprout into a wonderful tree that will bless everyone you know.

Overcome your Fear of Success!

One of my clients said to me yesterday that he is terrified of making a lot of money. I asked him why and he said that he is afraid that somehow it would change him and he might not stay as happy as he is now. He is happily married, with two children, and fears that somehow this might change if he made more money. His unusual self-honesty reveals a trait that many of us unconsciously harbor: the fear of success.

Yet if we are to live as spiritually free people in this world, we must be willing to transcend all fears–including those of success. If you are willing to be honest, you will probably see that somewhere within you there is a fear of great success. A fear that perhaps you would really change, and perhaps wouldn't honor your friends or your marriage as you did when you had less money.

The way to overcome these fears is to realize that you are really helping everyone in your world as you let a greater measure of success flow through your life. Then your world can benefit everyone else through increased jobs, generosity, and all the possibilities that prosperity creates.

You must saturate your awareness with the idea that prosperity is good, success is good, and that living in limitation serves no person. As you accept this into your awareness, you will find that new ideas begin to pop into your mind that open up the possibility for great success and happiness.

The day will come when you will look back and wonder why you didn't start your new ideas sooner! But at least you will have the satisfaction that you did take action, and you did create the dreams that lived in your heart. So start today, this very minute, and begin moving in the direction of a richer, more prosperous existence in this world. Everyone will be glad you did!

Summary and Action Plan

1. A rich prosperous life benefits all people. As you prosper, you serve everyone in your life.

2. If you really want to prosper you must be willing to overcome the limiting programming you may have picked up about prosperity.

3. You do no favor to the world by living a limited life. All good has come from people willing to dream big and create beautiful things.

4. A prosperous life is a life rich with plenty of time, good health, good friends, and plenty of money for every good need and desire. It is a balanced life, one that is free from compulsion.

Exercise:

Take a piece of paper and draw a line down from top to bottom in the middle.

A. On the left side write quickly, without thinking, what you have heard about money and success. Be honest about your feelings.

B. Then on the right side of the paper write down what you now believe, not what you were programmed to believe. If you believe prosperity is good write it down. If you think money serves everyone, write it down.

C. Put down every reason why prosperity is good, and why the world would be a better place if you increased your measure of prosperity. Remember, until you are sold on the value of being prosperous, it won't happen for you!

Chapter 4

Discover a World of Boundless Opportunity

At this very moment, exactly where you are, you are surrounded by boundless opportunity! It does not matter your circumstance, your past mistakes, what you have or have not done. You are living in a field of infinite awareness, unlimited possibilities. All that remains is for you to awaken to the potential that surrounds you, to open your eyes that you might see.

The great mystery of this world is why so few people see, why so few people really begin to walk the high road of total freedom. But you are one of those people that has chosen freedom. That is why you have drawn this book into your life. This is why you are taking the time to truly examine your own life.

One Idea Can Totally Change Your Life!

Did you know it takes only one idea to totally change your life? One idea can bring you all the prosperity you dream of. One idea can bring you the happiness that you aspire to. Your mind is the source of unlimited ideas. Not a single scientist has ever found any limit on the human mind to generating ideas.

Today we live in a world filled with miraculous inventions that even 100 years ago would have seemed beyond all possibility. Yet today we zoom around in jet aircraft, type on computers as small as books, and use miniature wireless phones to call all over the world. The list goes on and on. Each of these inventions began in the human mind.

What ideas are waiting in your mind right now, waiting to bring you greater good than you ever imagined? Are you willing to honor your own ideas? Or do you just discard your own ideas considering them of little value? Only when you begin to honor your own mind, your own ideas, your own vision of this world will you ever be free.

Opportunity is Where you Are Right Now!

It is so easy to start believing that opportunity was greater at another time, or is easier for other people. But the opportunity you need to make your life become truly fulfilled surrounds you right now. There is infinite perfection that surrounds you and uplifts you at this very moment.

Become like a child searching for the miracles, the new ideas, the new perspectives that will transform your own life right now. Cultivate a child like curiosity towards everything in your world. Learn how things work, learn why people act the way they do. Learn what effect you have on others.

Learn what effect other people have on you. Who makes you feel better about yourself? Who makes you feel like a success, a good person, a healthy human being? Spend time with those people. You are entitled to success, a good life–a life of rich ever expanding expressions of fulfillment.

Become aware of everything in your environment. Which environments make you feel more alive, more fulfilled? Which thoughts uplift you and make you feel as though you can do anything? Consciously move your life towards great expressions of freedom, choice and responsibility.

Learn to take responsibility for how your life got to where it is right now. What choices did you make (and are you continuing to make) that caused you to arrive where you are? No matter how wonderful your life is right now, you can walk to higher planes of joy, peace and freedom.

The wonderful thing about your life is that as you awaken to new vistas of opportunity, you will awaken many others as well. For this is the great miracle of life: as the sea of opportunity rises in your world, it raises many other boats as well. As you learn to think positively, finding opportunity everywhere, other people will be inspired as well. Soon you will find a multiplying, magnifying force of good radiating in and through your world, touching everyone you know.

Success: Seeing Opportunity Where Others See Limitation

As you gaze upon the world, what do you see? Do you see unlimited possibilities to accomplish good? Or do you get discouraged by all the problems that appear in the world? It is easy to get discouraged. All of us face the same challenge. It is hard to face the poverty, the suffering that many people experience, and still believe in a good, healthy, happy world. Yet this is exactly what you must do if you wish to walk the high road–serving the world, and awakening to yourself.

You see until you can rise above the appearance of limitation–both in your life and the world as a whole– you will never be able to make a true contribution. Only when you can become a magnet for prosperity, peace and happiness, a generator of joy and freedom, can you really contribute to the world.

He Created Thriving Business, where Others Saw No Opportunity

Consider this example of seeing opportunity where another did not. A friend of mine owns a bed and breakfast in Vermont. They allowed a man to manage the property. His compensation would come from the profits he generated from the business. Even though his intentions were good, the man always said that business was not adequate to generate an income from the property. He repeatedly said that the opportunity was too limited, and he wasn't able to earn a decent income. Finally, he gave notice and moved away because he said the potential didn't exist to earn the income he needed.

A new manager came in, the exact same age as the prior manager. Within two months the new manager had generated more profits than the prior manager had in the entire prior year. He soon developed a thriving business capable of supporting his family.

Where the old manager had seen limitation and lack, the new manager saw opportunity and unlimited possibilities. Because he saw that possibility he brought it into reality. What is so important about this lesson is that it was the very same property, in the same economy, same time period, separated only by two months. Yet the new awareness created an entirely different set of possibilities that led to a rich expression of prosperity and opportunity.

You can do the same thing in your life! We have all missed opportunities in our lives. The important thing is to focus on your present, exactly where you are and begin looking for the hidden opportunities that await you!

This, then, is your assignment if you truly wish to walk the high road: rise above all appearances. See opportunity where others see none. See the possibility of abundance where only poverty appears. Bestow health on those that suffer. Bestow peace on those that worry. Know that there are answers for every problem, solutions for every condition. Decide that you are a part of the answer, and give up being part of the problem. Dare to live an outrageously good life, and leave behind all guilt, negativity and limitation. Behold this world as a heaven, and see God's work present at all times. Help people remember who they are, and the true potential that they have for freedom. Throw off the shackles of limited thinking, the chains of negativity. Arise to the infinite power of your own relationship to this magnificent creation called life. Drink from the source of continual renewal, and experience the vigor of an ever expanding, more joyous life.

As you learn to walk on the high road, your life becomes a blessing to all. Allow the blessing to expand, to multiply until your cup overflows with good. Then you truly will be serving God's purpose for your life.

Summary and Action Plan

1. Learn to see opportunity all around you. At this very moment, everything is present to unfold unlimited opportunity in your world.

2. Learn to see opportunity where others see limitation. Become child like and search for opportunity everywhere.

3. See answers present for every condition in your life and the world.

4. Dare to become truly happy, truly prosperous without guilt. Your happiness will become a blessing to all.

Exercise:

A. List 10 things for which you are grateful right now about your life and the world you live in.

B. List 10 ways you could take advantage of the opportunities in your world right now.

C. List the people and places that make you the happiest, most fulfilled. For 30 days, spend as much time as you can surrounding yourself by these people, and going to these places. At the end of 30 days there will be no returning to your old ways.

D. List the negative habits you would like to give up.

E. List the positive habits you would like to develop.

F. Remember: you will succeed!

Chapter 5

You Can Have the Relationship of Your Dreams!

You can have fabulous, inspired relationships. They can be a source of fulfillment, lasting happiness and peace in your life. Harmony, prosperity, and wonderful opportunities can come to you if you acquire simple, easy to learn relationship skills.

Isn't it strange that in our society, where relationships seem to be more precarious than ever, there is very little taught in schools about how to have a long lasting, happy relationship. Yet the steps to be taken are really quite easy, and the reward is great.

As an attorney I have performed over 1,000 divorces. I have also had the chance to counsel many married couples. I have always asked people why they are getting divorced, and also what allows successful relationships to continue. The ideas shared in this chapter come from observing these people, and from my own life.

Learn to Love Unconditionally!

We all want to be loved and accepted. We spend much of our lives looking for this love. Yet the great paradox of this world is that if we really want love we must be willing to give up searching for it!

Love is something that comes to us only as we learn to express the love that we seek. As we learn to unconditionally love, we will find that unconditional love comes into our world.

Unfortunately, we have all been exposed to the mutual need fulfillment approach to relationships. Simply put, this means two people come together not out of love, but rather out of a desire to "get" something from the other person, whether love, sex, or money.

The problem with mutual need fulfillment is that it has nothing to do with love. It encourages people to approach marriage and significant relationships from the point of view of mutual bargaining: you give me what I want, and I will give you what you want. When I say, "I love you," then you must say it in return.

This approach to relationships can never give us what we are looking for. We want love, acceptance and joy from another. Yet, by conditioning our love on the other person's performance we deny that love to the other. Naturally, we will not get what we deny to the other person in the relationship.

Only when we can experience the natural love that exists within our own heart towards other human beings can we build the foundation that will truly lead to a life of fulfilling, joyous relationships.

The great miracle is that love is our natural state. When we allow the walls to dissolve between us we will discover love begins to flow and bring forth happiness in every part of our lives.

Give up your conditions, your demands, even if just for a week, or a day, and discover the beauty of granting unconditional love to your partner. You will be delighted by the joy that enters you heart. If you do this for even 1 week, I assure your relationship will never be the same again!

Become Vulnerable: Give Up the Need for Protection

In order to love unconditionally, we must give up the fear of loss. As long as we are devoting our energy to protecting ourselves from hurt, we cannot truly express unconditional love.

He took a Chance and Ended Up in a Very Happy Marriage

A friend of mine had been in a relationship that ended in a painful divorce. For a while after his divorce he was careful when he was dating women, always attempting to screen and make sure they were right for him.

He went out of his way to tell the women he dated that he wasn't interested in a long-term relationship. Not surprisingly, his relationships never developed into any depth. Eventually, he realized that the only way he could proceed was to quit trying to protect himself from loss.

He also decided that he could take a chance going out with women that didn't necessarily fit his pre-conceived expectations.

What do you think happened? As he became more flexible, more vulnerable he met a beautiful woman who really was quite different than he would have expected.

For some reason there was a bond between the two of them, and the relationship grew more serious to the point he decided to get married. He has been married a number of years now and is one of the happiest people I know, with several children. He would be the first to tell you that it would never have happened if he had not been willing *to take a chance!*

His story illustrates a very simple lesson: *your happiness in relationships is directly related to your ability to let go and become vulnerable.* True love and happiness exists only in a state of surrender, of release. If you feel you must remain in control, you will never be able to discover the joy of being in a close relationship.

Become Your Own Soul Mate!

No other person can ever make you happy! Only you can make yourself happy. This simple truth is the key to finding great happiness in all of the relationships that you choose.

If you really want to have a lifetime of happy, fulfilling relationships, including a wonderful marriage, then you must learn to find happiness within yourself. It is an extraordinarily simple idea, yet is the only path to lasting happiness.

We have all been raised on the myth that we will fall madly in love with someone and that person will transform a dull life into a magical, happy experience. So (usually in adolescence) we start looking for the one and only.

We then find someone, fall madly in love, have a few years of great joy, and then all-too-often get divorced. Why does this happen? I wondered about this myself, and realized that in my role as a divorce lawyer there was a unique opportunity for insight.

After interviewing thousands of people involved in divorces, there is one striking lesson that stands out. *We must not look to our spouse as our source of happiness or we will certainly end up disillusioned, and probably divorced.*

For so many people the initial infatuation gives them a tremendous rush of happiness. Naturally they want more of this, and decide to get married. Then nature plays what might appear to be a cruel trick: those wonderful chemicals that give rise to that glorious "in love" feeling wear off.

For most people the initial chemicals that give rise to infatuation wear off somewhere between 2-4 years. It is about that time people start wondering what they ever saw in their spouse.

After the chemicals wear off, the people show up in my office to get divorced, saying things like "I never really loved him (or her.)" Actually, most people were in love, and wanted to be with each other *at the time they decided to be married.*

The problem, simply stated, is that after the infatuation wears off, each person is faced with two possibilities: decide it was all a mistake and move on to find another person that will give them a rush for a couple of years, or decide to learn to be truly happy from within, and cease looking for happiness in another human being. If this happens, then the marriage can begin to move on to truly great joy as a mutual journey through the life experience.

This is a fundamental shift in perception. You cease looking for another soul mate, and realize that you are your own soul mate. You discover that you have unlimited joy right within you and cease expecting everyone around you to make you happy.

It is incredible how happy a life can become when you discover the untapped wells of joy that lie right within your own mind, your own heart. You can actually learn to trigger and experience all of those wonderful chemicals of love from within your own body.

The great paradox of seeing yourself as your own soul mate is you are then permitted to have a wonderfully happy, fulfilling relationship. Why? Because you are no longer putting on the other person the impossible burden of making you happy. You are taking responsibility for your own happiness; and, in so doing create the possibility for a truly long lasting, ecstatic relationship.

I am not suggesting that there are never reasons for completing relationships. You must look to your own inner guidance to learn whether it is appropriate to continue building a relationship with someone, or to complete it. But the miracle of life is that if you decide to continue building, you can create wonderful joy by discovering the happiness within your own soul.

There Will Always Be Someone When You Are Ready!

You are a powerful creator. Your words, thoughts and deeds are weaving your destiny from moment to moment. Yet many people start to despair that they will ever find someone to spend their lives with.

Having counseled many people and studied relationships intensively, I am personally convinced that no person has to go through this life alone if they don't want to. *If you are open to a wonderful relationship, you can have one.*

How are you going to create this relationship? First, remember that you don't need anyone for your happiness! Remember that you have an unlimited power to create happiness and fulfillment. Then set about becoming the happiest person you could imagine being.

You will become a Magnet

Learn to radiate happiness at all times, wherever you are. Soon you will be attracting like a powerful magnet. People will be attracted to your wonderful vibrancy and vitality.

You will find that you have more attention than you know what to do with! Then you will have a new problem, how to decide who you are going to spend your time with.

Woman Minister Marries Young Man

One of the great lessons that taught me there is always a right person for each of us came from one of my spiritual teachers.

She was a beautiful, very heavy person. She had become so heavy that physical mobility had become very difficult. She was in her 50s at the time I met her.

Soon after, that time she met a man that was 20 years younger than her. He felt a tremendous love and devotion for her and, after waiting for a considerable period of time, they married. He was a very handsome, attractive man.

People sometimes used to be surprised that a young, handsome man would choose to be with a woman that was considerably older and heavy as well. Yet as I came to know them both, I understood the deep love that existed between them, and the sincerity of their relationship.

Her husband saw the wonderful spiritual love that she emanated and that became his vision of her. This is a story with a happy ending. They stayed married for many years until her death a number of years later! I will always be grateful to have witnessed the power that love has to overcome differences of all kinds.

Unlock Your Natural Charisma and Beauty!

You are a beautiful, attractive person expressing the very perfection of life. Does that seem like an exaggeration to you? We have all been saturated with Madison Avenue images of what is supposed to represent beauty and attractiveness.

Yet true charisma and beauty are not based on looking like some stereotyped image. We all know those who don't seem to fit the conventional image of beauty yet attract others constantly. On the other hand there are people that dress the right way, drive the right kind of car, and never seem to be able to find the relationships they seek. Why is this?

The answer, quite simply, is that true charisma arises only when you discover your own inner magnificence. When you truly learn to love yourself and experience the wonder of life people will feel that right away.

When you spend time with a charismatic person you go away feeling better about yourself and your life. You feel lifted up, rather than weighted down.

Always remember: true charisma–true beauty–has nothing to do with how your physical body looks! Never compare yourself with another person. Instead, radiate your own natural beauty, love and light, and you will find that you have become extraordinarily attractive to people. This is true regardless of your weight or any other physical trait. You are beautiful just as you are. Awaken to that truth!

Use Your Magic Wand to Create a Magical Relationship

Once you realize that you are the source of your own happiness, you can begin to create extraordinarily happy relationships. I have had the good fortune of officiating at a number of weddings in my role as a minister.

I always tell the newlywed couples to use their magic wand to create a magical relationship. How do you do this? Always speak and think positively about your husband or wife. Tell everyone what a thoughtful, loving person your spouse is–even at those times when it seems to be a slight exaggeration!

Make a point of telling your spouse every day how great he or she is. Be grateful for all of the little things that are so easily overlooked. Give compliments freely.

We all tend to fulfill the expectations of people around us. So, if you consistently expect the best from your spouse, you will be amazed to see that you will not be disappointed over time.

Remember: you are a magical, powerful being, capable of directing and scripting your life. Be willing to script your relationship, and create a marriage that goes beyond your most wonderful expectations.

Focus on What Works in the Relationship!

If we want to have truly long lasting, happy relationships, we must focus on the good in the relationship, rather than the problems. We all have a tendency to want to focus on problems thinking that in so doing we will solve them.

This seems perfectly logical, and perhaps–in some areas of life–is correct. But in the arena of relationships the rules are reversed.

In this magical kingdom we *create* what we think about. So if we continue thinking about our partner's deficiencies, what we will notice is that the problems simply persist. We must think, dwell and focus on what is good, on what is right in the relationship, and leave the rest alone.

If you really do this you will be amazed by the results. You will find that the problems that once seemed so important will begin to disappear! *Could it really be so easy?* Yes, but only if you can *really* let go of the negative and begin to dwell on the positive.

Marriage Saved by Focusing on Good Qualities

John and Cynthia had been married less than a year, but as often is the case, they were having difficulty adapting to the changed world of married life. They were arguing about the location of things in the house, about their dogs, which were getting into fights regularly, and many other things.

The criticisms and ego battling continued constantly. Things were going from bad to worse. First, they would start discussing a problem area, but then it would degenerate into mutual criticisms, leading to withdrawal and silence. A downward spiral was occurring.

John spoke with me about the situation and was very concerned that the marriage might not succeed unless some change occurred. I suggested that he quit worrying about the things that were bothering him, and instead focus on things that had originally brought them both together. I told him that he had to let go completely his focus on the problems and dare to proceed in faith that a change could occur.

The results were nothing short of miraculous. The marriage turned around within 30 days! John discovered that when he quit criticizing Cynthia, she had much greater goodwill, and also stopped attacking him. Then he noticed that a spirit of flexibility and compromise entered the relationship. Both he and Cynthia were willing to be flexible and giving.

I have kept in touch with John and Cynthia over the years (it has now been 13 years), and they are one of the happiest couples I know. They have four beautiful children, three dogs, and are able to live in great harmony. People that know them frequently comment on how lucky they are to have a good relationship.

Their marriage was saved by practicing the central theme of this book: you can change your life by changing what you think and speak about. They directed their creative energies into creating what they wanted. They gave up thinking about and dwelling on their problems. By doing this they literally created a magnificent future for themselves. *You can do the same thing!*

Be Flexible Like the Bamboo Tree!

The Chinese have a saying that the strongest tree is the bamboo because it is the most flexible. It is much the same in a marriage or any other relationship. If you want it to last, and grow into a beautiful experience, then you must be willing to be very flexible.

No two human beings are alike. We all have tremendous differences, in our tastes, our goals, and in what we expect from a relationship. If you really need to do things your own way, it is probably better not to get married, or involved in a serious relationship.

Warning! If you truly wish to have a happy marriage, you, not your spouse, must be flexible! You cannot turn this principle around and expect your spouse to be flexible and compliant to your needs. Only true willingness to give and be flexible on your part will give you want you want.

Take Responsibility for 100% of the Relationship

Your relationship will really begin to take off when you see yourself as responsible for the whole relationship, *not just your part.* This means that when compromise is called for you will not wait for the other person to compromise–you will take the first step.

When you are taking responsibility for the whole relationship, you won't sit back and compare constantly to see who is doing more of what. Instead you will step in to do what needs to be done. As you do this, you will experience inner peace in your heart.

If an apology needs to be made you won't sit back and wait for the other person to apologize. Instead, you will take the action first, even if you don't feel you were wrong. This type of proactive behavior will eliminate most problems before they even arise.

Your Differences are Wonderful

Many times an obstacle to a happy marriage is the misplaced idea that you must be exactly alike. In most successful marriages I have observed there are tremendous differences between the people involved.

If you wish your marriage to succeed, learn to celebrate your differences instead of seeing them as an obstacle. Give up the illusion that you are supposed to be exactly alike and you will find that happiness will come to you much more quickly.

The perfection of this wonderful universe often draws people together that they may supplement each other. If you are exactly alike what supplementation could occur? But when you are different the scope of your experience can greatly expand.

Make it a practice to grant complete space, complete acceptance of the differences that exist between you. Honor the fact that you are each unique creations of the universe and have different needs, desires, and goals. If you can do this, then you will be practicing the unconditional love discussed earlier. You will find that as you grant "space" to your partner, you will get it back in equal measure.

Consider this idea: As we become more self-assured in who we are and what we believe, we really don't need everyone around us to give us agreement all the time. To put it another way, we can accept different points of view without always trying to convince everyone of our "rightness." This principle applies to all kinds of relationships. The closer the relationship, the more important it is.

Use Courtesy and Respect!

You can transform your relationships by learning to give courtesy and respect at all times. Why is it that people will often treat a complete stranger with greater respect and courtesy than the people that are closest in their lives? It is as if we have one face for public and another for those closest to us.

Nothing could be more damaging to any relationship than continually criticizing or putting down the other person. Yet many relationships digress into a spiral of traded criticisms. Each person is always looking for a chance to put the other down. Of course, it doesn't take a genius to see that these types of relationships usually end in my office as divorce cases.

On the other hand, no matter what has happened in the past you can transform your relationship by going out of your way to be polite. Think of how you treated your spouse when you first met. In most cases, you were probably very polite, sensitive, and compassionate. If you will think back you will probably also see that your spouse was treating you the same way.

This is the key. If either one of you starts treating the other with courtesy and respect, then the other will begin to respond in the same way. It will create a wonderful mutually reinforcing cycle of ascending love. A spirit of flexibility and happiness will enter the relationship.

A wonderful side benefit to treating each other with respect is that many of your original feelings will arise again, and you will feel like you are falling in love over again.

Every principle discussed in this chapter applies to all kinds of relationships–not just marriages or intimate relationships. The simple fact is that the quality of our lives in this world depends almost exclusively on our ability to master our relationships. If we learn to grant happiness to the people in our world we can come to know lasting peace, prosperity and happiness. This applies to every kind of relationship, whether it be work, friendship or otherwise.

Summary and Action Plan

1. You are an attractive, radiant being, capable of bestowing unconditional love on the people in your world.

2. As you learn to give love unconditionally, you will find that people are drawn into your life effortlessly.

3. The right relationship will appear in your world if you remain open. Don't allow your preconceived pictures to prevent you from seeing the beauty of the relationships that come to you.

4. Learn to give respect, to give love, and you will find love and respect pouring into your world from expected and unexpected places.

5. Focus on the best in your relationships, and the problems will take care of themselves. Quit worrying about the problems!

View all relationships as a blessings from God, and they will be!

Exercise:

A. Practice looking in the mirror and saying to yourself some like this: "You are a wonderful, charismatic, radiant being. You are attractive to people you meet, and bring happiness to all in your world." Repeat this every day for 30 days when you wake up and before you go to bed.

B. If you are in a serious relationship make a list of all the things you appreciate about the person. Then make a point of telling the person at least one of those things every day. Make sure that your comments are genuinely positive and not designed to manipulate. When you communicate from your heart good will come.

C. Make a point of giving a compliment to someone you don't know at least once a day. For example, you can thank the grocery store cashier for doing a good job. You can tell someone that they are dressed nicely. This exercise will move you beyond any natural shyness you may have and begin to open up your relationships.

D. If there is someone you want to get to know better ask the person to lunch, or at a minimum call him/her. Make a list of people that would enrich your life, and start reaching out to them to get to know them. Practice overcoming your fear of rejection.

Chapter 6

Access Your Creative Power to Fulfill Your Dreams!

This book is dedicated to empowering you to attain your dreams. The door in your mind has opened to infinite intelligence, which is now guiding you to your good this very second. In this chapter you will be given a number of tools designed to *open doors for you in accomplishing your dreams and goals. Each of these tools is designed to open up the channels in your mind to your infinite intelligence, the gateway that makes all things possible.*

While reading this chapter, keep this thought in mind: you may already know about the benefits of physical exercise, but you have to *actually exercise* to get the health benefits. The same is true with the information being shared here. In order to gain the benefits of these powerful tools, you must actually use them in your life. That is why actual examples are included, to give you a strong inner conviction of the reality and power of this approach.

Learn the Secret of Empowered Visualization

Many people have heard that visualization is a powerful technique for bringing things into your life. But people often fail to succeed using visualization. This is because they have not learned the secret of full, multi-dimensional visualization.

In the purest sense, visualization is simply bringing to your conscious mind vivid pictures and images of what you choose to create. I have found, both in my own experience, and that of many people I have known, the following steps will increase the likelihood of success.

Use Vivid multi-sensory Images

While you are seeing the chosen image in your mind's eye, it is important to involve all of the senses. Hear people talkin to you about your experience. Touch the objects of your visualization in your mind's eye. Smell anything in the room. In other words, involve all of your senses just as you would in any real-life experience. One great way to create a multi-sensory visualization is to write a *script* of one day of your life, as it will be after your goal has been realized. Consider this example:

> *Example: I am sitting on my patio, looking out over a beautiful vista. The wind is gently blowing through the trees. I can hear a wind chime ringing. I am a successful writer, and public speaker. My books are best sellers, and there is great demand for me to speak. I receive great fees, and my main challenge is to decide which engagements to accept. My prosperity is greater than I ever imagined, and continues to grow. My phone rings, and it is another top company requesting me to address its employees. I check my calendar, quote my fee, and*

*we finalize the deal. I have all the time I want with
my family. It is all great fun!*

You can see how this example could be more and more
finely detailed. The more detail, the better. You will find it a very
enjoyable experience. Best of all you will be bringing the picture
into your life faster than you could imagine. Read on in this chapter
to see how people just like you persisted in seeking their dreams,
and attained great success.

See Related Consequences of Attaining Your Goal

When you actually attain your dreams, all sorts of
consequences will come to pass in your life. If your dream is to be
a successful writer, imagine going to mail box to pick up letters
stating publishers' interest in your work. Imagine going to book
signings for interested readers. Imagine people coming up to you
and asking how to become a successful writer. In other words, all
of these things may come to pass as a result of the one primary
goal, and by visualizing them you create a greater sense of reality
in your mind.

Involve Other People in Your Imagery

If you are married, or have close friends, you can have the
other person jointly visualize the desired outcome. In the same
example of wishing to be a successful writer, you could jointly
visualize your book sitting on the best seller stack in the local
bookstore. Every time you go to the store for any purpose you both
can visualize the book already being published. Just for fun,
imagine yourself tapping someone on the shoulder and saying that
you wrote the book (as they stare at you in disbelief!).

Speak About Your Dream as If It is Already Realized

This is the same principle that I used to create a successful business. Just speak as if you are already in possession of the visualized dream. This will tend to encourage you to take the action necessary to bring it into reality.

Take Action!

The entire purpose of visualization is to motivate you to believe in yourself, in your ability to accomplish your dream. You can visualize all you want, but if you fail to take any action, your dream is not likely to happen. On the other hand, if you believe in your dream, know it is only a matter of time before it will occur, then you will take all the steps to make it happen. Just as importantly, the unlimited power of the infinite consciousness will go before to prepare the way causing your actions to bear fruit!

Ask for Divine Guidance for All of Your Dreams!

It has been said that we must be careful about what we wish for because we may get it. For that reason it is very important to turn your dream over to God, and for that which will be the highest and best outcome for all concerned. That way you are really asking for infinite intelligence to guide your way, and only good things can come to you.

I have listed some amazing examples below of people that have used these techniques in their visualizations with miraculous results. Each of these stories is true, just as your story will be!

These People Used Empowered Visualization To Attain Their Dreams

New Car Won Through Visualization

A good friend of mine used this system of empowered visualization to win a Radio Giveaway contest. He heard that a certain model car was to be given away. Naturally, there were a great number of participants.

This is the way the contest worked: people that called and got through would become part of a finalist group. That finalist group would be allowed to reach into a jar and pull out one of hundreds of keys. If that key worked in the ignition of the car the contestant would win.

Naturally, the large number of callers and the great number of keys to be drawn from made the odds of any person winning very small. But my friend had been studying the power of visualization and made a very conscious experiment, which embodies the secrets of empowered visualization.

First, through persistent calling, he got himself into the finalist group. Then, he set about getting a full multi-sensory experience of what it would be like to own the car. The car was on display at a local dealer. He would go there frequently to look at it and sit in it.

He wasn't allowed to start it, but he frequently asked for the trunk key so he could open the trunk. This way he would have the experience of turning the key in the lock, and impressed it on his mind.

At home he repeatedly visualized himself in the radio station, going over to the container of keys, pulling a key out, sitting down in the car and starting it! He talked to his Wife about what they would do with the car after they won it. Even she thought he had gone off the "deep end."

Finally, the day came for him to go down to the radio station with the other 100 finalists. All 100 drew numbers to determine the order they would get to pick a key from the jar. He pulled number 78 from the jar. At first he was crestfallen, thinking his chances of winning were eliminated. Then he decided to retain faith, and trust that he would still win anyway.

One by one, the other contestants went up to the jar, pulled out a key, and tried to start the car—and failed. Then it was his turn. He reached into the jar and chose a key (they were all identical in appearance). He walked over to the car, turned the key in the ignition and it started! The engine roared to life, and he won his car!

When he told me about this experience, he was, of course, thrilled. He had consciously set out to test the power of visualization. He had been reading books on visualization, and used this as his experiment. He carried the process through in complete detail. And it worked! He did manifest his vision.

He embodied the all the steps of empowered visualization:

1. He got a rich, multi-sensory experience of his desired outcome by going to the lot and sitting in the car;

2. He contemplated the consequences of having the car by checking into the insurance and various options available to him;

3. He involved his wife in his visualization;

4. He talked about it as though it was a reality.

Writing & Mail Order Business Started!

An amazing example of our power to create through visualization occurred to an author I know. He had lived the majority of his life as an equipment salesman. But he, like most of us, had a dream of greater prosperity and freedom.

Something within him made him feel that he could write and speak on positive themes. You must understand that he had no experience doing this whatsoever. He decided he would start by visualizing himself as a successful writer and speaker. He saw himself standing in front of groups speaking. He imagined his writing appearing in newspapers and books.

Additionally, he started visualizing receiving checks in the mail. He saw himself going down to the mail box and seeing it filled with checks, all made out to him. He practiced seeing this in his mind over and over again. Whenever his wife picked up the mail, he would ask her if the checks were arriving yet (mind you, he had hadn't even started a business venture!). He jokingly says that his wife and children thought he was a little crazy.

He continued this visualization process over and over again. Then, through a totally unplanned set of events, he got the opportunity to write a positive thinking column in a weekly paper. The column was supposed to be temporary, but it became very popular. As its popularity grew, people would occasionally ask him whether he had reprints of the articles.

One day he made a note in his column that reprints were available for a small price, and listed his home address. What do you think happened? Shortly after that, he went to the mail box and it was stuffed full of envelopes, all with checks made out to him!

His vision had become reality. *Stop. Let it in.* He had no background, no prior experience, no history of success in the writing field. Yet, the vision that he had imagined so vividly over and over again had become completely true, within a period of a few short years.

After that time he started speaking before various groups on positive themes, just as he had imagined. He eventually wrote a book as well.

His story is a perfect example of empowered visualization. He saw in his mind the primary goals, speaking in front of a group, or publishing his work. Additionally, he saw secondary effects, such as going to the mail box to pick up his checks. Finally, he involved other people in his vision by asking his wife and children about the checks.

By combining all of these techniques, he created a fully integrated vision in his own mind. He saw it as an accomplished reality, which brought the vision into reality in his world.

Could it really be that simple? Yes! Life is much simpler than we normally think, but few of us ever take the time to use the power we have been given. We spend far too much of our time dwelling on problems; personal, political, you name it. In so doing, we deny ourselves the chance to really move in the direction of our dreams.

Contemplate for a moment what you think about on a daily basis. How often are your thoughts positive, filled with powerful, exciting visions of your future? How much of your mental energy is devoted to creating wonderful new adventures of love, peace and prosperity. The choice is yours–why don't you start today! You will be amazed by the results that rapidly come into your life.

Mortgage Paid Through Visualization!

Another friend of mine used this technique to pay off the mortgage on his house. Like most people, the prospect of paying off the full mortgage seemed somewhat daunting, since it requires a large sum of cash all at once.

Nonetheless, he and his wife tried this experiment. Whenever they were driving somewhere together they would practice visualizing themselves walking into the mortgage office and paying off the mortgage. Then they saw themselves taking their children to the local children's pizza restaurant, buying a role of tokens and celebrating payment of the mortgage.

They practiced this visualization, talked about how much fun it would be to go to the restaurant with their children, and experienced it as a complete reality that was sure to come to pass. They thought of it much like you might plan to go to a movie on Saturday night. They would take turns describing the events in great detail. They did this regularly between 30-40 times. Then they released the matter, and frankly didn't think about it very often.

Approximately 1 year later, through a set of highly unusual circumstances, he closed some major unexpected deals that provided them with the cash necessary to pay off the mortgage. They paid it off, went to the pizza restaurant and celebrated, exactly as they had visualized it!

The time from inception of the vision, to manifestation as a reality was approximately 14 months. Their goal had been to do it in 12 months, a 2-month margin of error!

This example illustrates the different steps of visualization. They didn't just visualize the house being paid for. They also saw themselves celebrating as a result of it occurring. They involved their children in the vision so that it would have a complete reality to their minds. They also shared the vision back and forth, to create a shared mind awareness of the vision.

Use a Creativity Board to Manifest Your Dreams

One of the simplest and yet effective tools I have come across for accessing the creative mind is the creativity board. A creativity board is a cork board where you can put pictures and slogans that stimulate your mind and embody your goals.

During my seminars we often make creativity boards, using old magazines, newspapers, or any other source of literature. I enjoy using advertisements that come in the mail because they often have very positive slogans on them. Whatever the source, make sure the pictures and words excite you, and are things you would like to create in your own life.

The board should be put in a place where you can see it on a daily basis. Also you should constantly keep updating the board with new pictures and statements. This keeps the interaction with your mind dynamic, and maximizes the brain interaction. It involves the imaging part of your mind, what is referred to as the "right brain."

This system of putting up a board may seem simplistic, but has been used by major companies with great success. For example Disneyland puts proposed projects into "story" boards. This becomes part of a brainstorming technique to determine what projects to move forward on. If it works for Disney, it can work for you!

In the courses I have taught over the years I have seen amazing results from this seemingly simple tool.

Wife Met!

One of the most dramatic examples I personally have experienced involved meeting my own wife. I was at my barber getting my hair cut when I saw a picture of a woman on a calendar (no it wasn't a pinup!).

Something in the face of the woman was appealing to me so I asked him whether I could have the picture, planning to put it on my creativity board. He said that as soon as the month was up I could do so.

Sure enough, when I was there for my next haircut, he said I could have the photograph. So I went home and put it on my creativity board. Less than one month later I was at a party where I started talking to an intelligent young woman. We hit it off immediately and started dating.

Imagine my surprise when she came to our first date dressed in an almost identical outfit to the woman on the creativity board: the color of the dress, the necklace, and even the hair style were uncannily similar to the picture. Her eyes were the same color, and the hair was same color. When I showed her the picture, she also admitted there was a striking resemblance.

We got married a little more than a year later and now have four wonderful children! I keep the picture to remind me that we live in a magical world beyond our comprehension.

Did I have precognition and somehow see what she looked like before I met her? Or was she drawn into my reality because of the creativity board? In the final analysis it doesn't matter since the process works, as the following examples illustrate.

Woman Goes to China!

In the first seminar I taught years ago, a woman who was a housekeeper with a modest income, put down a picture of Hong Kong on her creativity board. She came to me proudly and stated that she would be traveling to China. I must admit that I was a little dubious when I saw the picture, but I was supportive.

Before the end of the year, she and I—as well as 15 others—traveled to Hong Kong together. Her picture had come into reality. What is critical for the reader to understand is that the trip to Hong Kong had never been thought of, or discussed at the time she put her picture on the board.

Tax Debt Eliminated.

Another woman came to me and asked how she should deal with a large tax liability of many thousands of dollars. She said she had already seen tax counsel, and didn't know what to do. Again, my rational mind kicked in, as I wondered whether a creativity board could really work against the IRS! Nonetheless I advised her to put a picture of the tax assessment with the word paid across it, and to forgive the IRS.

I forgot about the incident until several months later when she came to me and proudly held up a piece of paper showing a current balance owed to IRS of ZERO! The IRS had reviewed her tax situation again and concluded they had made a mistake. She was thrilled (as you might imagine)!

Roses and a Trip to Lake Tahoe!

A woman who took one of my recent seminars and is also my employee showed me her creativity board with a picture of a large vase of roses. Next to the roses was a beautiful picture of Lake Tahoe. *Three days later I walked into her office and there sat a beautiful vase of roses just like the picture.*

Within a month she was traveling to spend the weekend at Lake Tahoe! She had received a gift of trip to Lake Tahoe from a friend. What is important for the reader to understand is that she had no plans for Tahoe, nor was she expecting any flowers. Both of these events were wonderful surprises to her.

Use Self-Hypnosis

You can learn to use self-hypnosis as a powerful, creative tool to train, and strengthen your mind. One of the best ways to do this is immediately before you are going to sleep. Normally, for most people, the mind is unfocused while sleeping. But we can give directives before going to sleep that will have powerful influences on our life.

Think of certain suggestions you would like to give your mind as you are falling to sleep. You become very susceptible to suggestion at that time. Consider these possible examples:

I am completely invigorated and revitalized when I wake up.
When I wake up I will be happier than I ever have been.
Wonderful joy and peace fills my heart as I sleep, and when I wake up.
Creative answers come to me effortlessly for all parts of my life.
God protects and prospers me in all that I do.

These suggestions can be used either in the first person, as they are written or in the second person. For example, instead of saying "I am" in the different suggestions, simply state "You are." It is good for the mind to hear this in various ways. You will find the way that seems most empowering to you.

If you get in the habit of doing this when you are falling to sleep, it will become a very enjoyable process. I have been doing it for years, and it is part of my sleeping process. Feel free to give yourself whatever suggestions you feel are best for your life. All you are doing is stimulating your mind to create wonderful goodness in your life.

You will find that you can awaken with tremendous energy and vitality, simply because you have programmed this into your mind. Your mind will bring you what you want if you are willing to train it!

Summary and Action Plan

1. You have access to the infinite mind to bring your dreams into reality.

2. Use your power of visualization to access the infinite mind and speed your dreams into reality.

Exercise:

A. Take one or more of your dreams (listed in the prior chapter) and follow the steps for empowered visualization. Write a script, and do the other steps. Act in as much detail as the man who won his car. Soon you will be moving rapidly in the direction of your dreams.

B. Make a creativity board. You can buy a cork board at any stationery store, and most drug stores. Take old magazines and cut out the pictures and slogans you find exciting. Put the board in a place where you can see it daily, such as your closet door. You will be surprised over time when you see how many things you put down come into reality.

C. Use Self-Hypnosis to stimulate your mind. Your mind is an unlimited reservoir for new ideas. Self-Hypnosis is one of the valuable techniques you can use to bring the most out of your subconscious mind. Do it every night before you go to bed. You will awake feeling refreshed and happy.

Chapter 7

Prepare Yourself for Greatness!

Everything that happens to you, everything that you accomplish in this life is a direct result of the way you use your mind! You weave your destiny through the thoughts you entertain, the information you put into your mind, and the way you use it.

In short, the way you use your mind will determine whether you rise or fall, whether you succeed or fail, whether you are happy or unhappy. *Before you go on any further, stop and re-read this paragraph.* It holds the key to everything you want to attain in this life.

You have been given enormous power to mold and shape your destiny. But if you wish to elevate your life you must truly become vigilant. You must become completely aware of the patterns of your mind, the information you take into it, and the thoughts you continue to entertain. You must become dedicated to transforming the very way in which you use your mind.

In this chapter, you will be given the keys to using your mind in new and powerful ways that will unleash great potentiality.

You will see how to avoid the hypnotizing effect of limited thinking, so you can make the contribution you came to this earth to make.

Awaken from the Hypnotic Spell of Limitation!

If it is true that we have a tremendous capability to transform our lives, then why do so many people have lives of limitation and suffering? Quite simply, it is because the human mind can easily be *hypnotized* into limited, restricted thinking patterns. Once those patterns are established, they can be very hard to remove.

The term hypnosis, as I am using it here, refers to our natural tendency to unconsciously adopt limitations on our thinking, our expectations, and our view of life itself. These unconscious beliefs become *hidden chains* restricting our options, our choices, our goals and dreams.

Don't Be an Elephant!

A true story reveals how easily our minds can unconsciously adopt limitation. Every circus uses elephants in one way or another. This has always presented a problem because the elephants are so strong that if they ever got loose they could create havoc.

To avoid this problem a large, strong chain is placed around their legs when the elephants are small, preventing them from wandering off. When the young elephant tries to get away it feels the pain of the chain around its leg.

In time the elephant realizes the futility of trying to get away, and it *stops trying to do so*. Later, when the elephant is fully grown, all that is required to keep the massive, strong animal in place is the presence of a small chain around the leg. It doesn't even have to be anchored in place.

The elephant is actually free, *but it doesn't know it!* Why? Because the chain that used to exist around its leg is now located in a far more powerful location: *in the mind of the elephant*. As long as that elephant believes it is chained, it will be.

Have you stopped seeking your dreams because you don't believe they are possible? As long as you believe you cannot accomplish your dreams, then you *will* be right! You will not be able to accomplish them.

Your entire purpose is to resurrect your capability to dream again. You must begin to see that you can, in fact, accomplish your dreams. As you begin to believe again, you will find that energy, excitement and vitality surge back into you. You will feel young again, in love with everything! Dare to believe you can accomplish your dreams. What do you have to lose?

Don't be a Flat-World Thinker!

Consider for a moment Columbus' journey to the American Continent. For many thousands of years people were afraid to sail out into the oceans because they believed the world was flat. *They were afraid they would sail off the edge.* Even old maps showed dragons and other monsters devouring the people that sailed off the edge of the world.

This all sounds quaint and rather meaningless until you realize that the Flat World view had a tremendous limiting effect. When Columbus finally did make his journey it took only thirty-six days! Imagine! A journey of only 36 days was capable of separating two continents for thousands of years!

Can you see how easy it is to unconsciously adopt limiting beliefs? It is the beliefs you take for granted, the limits you assume are real that bind you. *In truth you are without limits, you have vast power. Do not let any other thought into your mind!*

If You Believe in Your Limitations, They Will Be Real!

You will find below a series of quotes, and examples of people who were hypnotized into limited thinking by the world around them. Instead of seeing opportunity, they saw limitation. Consider these amazing examples of limiting thinking, and how they were overcome when the thinking changed! *When you are reading these examples ask yourself how you, too, may be seeing the world through the filter of limitation. Open yourself to seeing the opportunities invisible to others.*

4-Minute Mile Said to be Impossible

For decades athletes were told that the human body could not run a mile under four minutes. It was said to be physically impossible. For a long time runners agreed with this assessment and never broke that barrier.

But one day–May 6, 1954–Roger Banister ran the mile in 3 minutes, 59.4 seconds. The news spread all over the world like wild fire. Less than six weeks later John Landy, of Australia ran the mile in only 3:58.0. Suddenly, runners everywhere realized that the 4-minute barrier could be broken. By the end of the 60s, there were over 200 people that had broken the 4-minute mile!

What happened? Did the runners suddenly become stronger? Did they suddenly develop some new power? Of course not! They were freed from the limitations of their own minds. The four-minute barrier existed in the mind of man, and nowhere else!

Telephone Considered Useless

"This 'telephone' has too many shortcomings to be seriously considered as a means of communication. The device is inherently of no value to us." Western Union internal memo, 1876.

Airplanes considered impossible

"Heavier-than-air-flying machines are impossible." Lord Kelvin, President, Royal Society, 1895. As we can all see today, Lord Kelvin was unbelievably limited in his thinking, yet the majority of people in his time would have agreed with him!

Patent Officer Says No New Inventions Possible after 1899

"Everything that can be invented has been invented." Charles H. Duell, commissioner U.S. Office of Patents, 1899. As we all know today, the not only was Charles Duell wrong, the exact opposite proved true: the greatest period of creativity and invention came after this statement. The airplane, telephone, radio, television,

computer, and phonograph–to mention just a few–were all invented after this statement!

Airplanes No Good for Military Use

"Airplanes are interesting toys, but of no military value. "Marshall Ferdinand Foch, professor of strategy, Ecole Superieure De Guerre. If he only knew, air superiority is now the determination of military success!

Radios Have No Value

"The wireless music box has no imaginable commercial value. Who would pay for a message sent to nobody in particular?" David Sarnoff's associates in response to his urging for investment in the radio of the 1920's. Radios have no value? Of course, today we know that many millionaires have been made from their radio businesses.

Talking Pictures Have No future

"Who the hell wants to hear actors talk?" Harry M. Warner, *Warner Brothers, 1927.* Of course we all know that "talking pictures" took over the market in almost no time. The actors that failed to make the transition lost their careers. Is there a change in your profession or career that will open up vast new opportunities as "talkies" did? Look around you, be open to the changes that are occurring. In those changes lies your opportunity for great success.

No Market for Computers in World

"I think there is a market for maybe five computers." Thomas Watson, Chairman of IBM 1943. Hard to believe he really said that!

No Reason for Computers in Home

"There is no reason for any individuals to have a computer in their home." Ken Olsen, president of Chairman and founder of the Digital Equipment Corp., 1977. Tell that to Microsoft! Bill Gates is a billionaire precisely because so many people do have computers!

The quotes and stories listed above illustrate a cardinal rule: As long as your believe in your limitations they will be real! What dream could you be working on that could unleash creativity, prosperity and happiness for yourself and others? Don't worry if it seems impossible, you may be the one to make it possible. (By the way, several of these examples came from an excellent article in Time Magazine, entitled "THE PAST, IMPERFECT" on July 15, 1996 Volume 148, No. 4.)

There is More opportunity than Ever Before!

As you can see from the preceding examples, we must all remain extremely careful not to accept the prevailing belief systems of the people around us. These beliefs are often far too limited, and will not take us in the direction of our dreams.

As Einstein said: "Genius is seeing what everyone else has seen, but thinking something *different*." If you really want to achieve success and fulfillment in this life you must be willing to look at your world as a place filled with boundless, unlimited opportunity.

You must be willing to condition your mind to expect and find opportunity under all circumstances. This requires the constant care, feeding, and nurturing of your mind. In the next section, you will learn how to rapidly reprogram your mind in order to create the success and fulfillment you truly deserve.

Remember: There is Always an Answer to the Challenge that Faces You!

Whenever you have a dream you want to attain or a problem you want to solve, it is critical to remember there is *always an answer! There is a way to get to your dream, your destination, but only if you can continue believing it.* You must be willing to cultivate this awareness, and let it saturate your mind. *You can accomplish your dreams; the answers and doorways do exist. But you must be willing to look for them!*

Learn to Think Like Thomas Edison!

Thomas Edison is one of the great minds of the modern era. He brought into existence many inventions that we take for granted today. The electric light bulb, the phone and the phonograph are just a few of the things that he played an instrumental role in inventing.

Yet how did he do it? Did you know that this man had only three months of formal schooling? He was actually dismissed from school; his mother was told that he had a learning disability. Can you imagine how different all of our lives would be if his mother had *believed* what the school told her? Surely she would have instilled that belief in Edison, and we would have never heard his name today.

Fortunately, his mother did *not* believe what the school told her. Instead she raised her boy to believe in his own abilities. As a result, he developed an amazing self-confidence (some called it arrogance!). When he set his mind on a goal, he didn't give up until he accomplished the goal. That is really what made him unusual.

The invention of the light bulb is an excellent example of how he persisted in the direction of his dreams. When he set out to invent the modern light bulb, the light bulb actually had already been invented. But all prior versions of the light bulb were just technological curiosities, costing as much as $10,000 in 19th century dollars (probably millions in today's dollars).

What made Edison different from other inventors was his belief, his *conviction,* that there was a way to create a reasonably priced light bulb. *He was unwilling to accept defeat or impossibility!*

So when it came to the light bulb, he declared to the newspapers that he would invent a practical, inexpensive light bulb within 18 months, *and he did so!* He failed over and over again, thousands of times, while perfecting his inexpensive light bulb. He tried all kinds of filaments, but finally came up with the idea of a vacuum inside the bulb.

The point is simple. He held the conviction in his mind that there was a way to create a long lasting, reasonably priced light bulb. If he had ever wavered in this belief he would have simply given up the project, and quit spending his money and time. He would have never achieved his goal. *How many times have you had an idea, or a dream, but given up because you thought you were being unrealistic? It is precisely that tendency we all have to give up in the face of adversity that we must overcome if we are to attain our dreams.*

He persisted until he got to his destination, and created the light bulb that we have all come to enjoy. Of course he followed this pattern with countless other inventions as well; he simply refused to accept defeat until he arrived at the desired goal.

By the way, it is well worth visiting his laboratory in Florida. Believe it or not, there are still light bulbs that he manufactured during his life *that have never burned out, and still function today! How's that for persistence!*

The light bulb story illustrates the key elements of the successful use of your mind: You must be willing to persist even though everyone else says it is impossible! You must *know* that there is an answer, invention, or goal waiting for you if you will just persist long enough. *Finally, you must be willing to use failure as a tool for success!*

Don't Overlook Your Answer

Many times the answer you seek is staring you right in the face. All that is required is a slight change in perspective, a shift in the way you look at your circumstances. Always assume that the answer you need, the new idea you want is right in front of you waiting for you to wake up and see it! If you aren't looking how are you going to find it?

Electricity Always There--A Power Waiting to be Harnessed!

Consider the discovery of electricity. For thousands of years people looked at a lightning storm, marveled at its beauty, but never realized the vast power it represented. They saw the lightning, but they didn't open their minds to the possibilities it represented. As Einstein would have said, they needed to see the lightning, but think something different.

So what happened? How did electricity finally get harnessed? People such as Benjamin Franklin began to think that maybe there was a power in that lightning, a power that could be harnessed. As many of you are probably aware, Franklin flew a kite with a key attached to it during a lightning storm. Fortunately, for him he wasn't electrocuted. But due to his experiment combined with others, the reality of this vast power began to be revealed.

Electricity had always been there, but people began to see new possibilities where previously they had only seen a natural phenomenon. Once the attitude changed it was only a matter of time before the vast possibilities of electricity were opened up. Electric lights, telephones, computers, water pumps, refrigerators, virtually every modern technology was created simply because people learned to use a power that had always been there. The answer was always there, but people had to see things in a different way to find it!

How often are we doing the same thing–staring at the answer but not seeing it? We must learn to look at our world with new, open eyes, constantly searching for the overlooked answer. If you get in the habit of looking all around for unseen opportunities, you will surely begin to find them. *Are you overlooking a vast power or new idea that could change your life for the better?*

Summary and Action Plan

1. Always remember the elephant, that great creature being limited by the chains that exist only in its own mind! Be constantly alert for limitations you may have unconsciously accepted in your own life.

2. There is always an answer, a solution to the challenge that faces you. Be willing to persist like Edison until you find it! Never doubt that the solution exists or you may stop looking for it!

3. The answer you seek, the idea that will transform your life is right in front you. Remember that millions of people were looking at lightning, but never saw its potential. You are probably looking right this second at your answers, the keys to fulfilling your dreams if you will just open your mind!

Exercise:

Practice looking at the circumstances of your life, just as they are, as the perfect place for you to attain your dreams, and find happiness. Instead of resisting, or resenting your current circumstances, see them as a blessing that will take you to the next level of joy, peace and happiness in your life. View each day like a game, looking for miracles, answers and ideas that will transform your life to greater peace, joy and prosperity.

Chapter 8

Use the Power of Synergy to Create Miracles

Synergy is a power that has the ability to greatly amplify your success and fulfillment in life. This is an age-old secret that has created great success and happiness for many people.

Andrew Carnegie used synergy and became the wealthiest man in the world. He gave away more for charitable purposes than most people ever owned! Today there are museums, libraries, and public buildings all made available to the public because of his generosity. Thomas Edison used synergy to bring forth countless inventions that benefit our lives today. Gandhi used synergy to gain independence for India. Synergy is at the core of all monasteries, ashrams, and churches.

So what exactly is synergy, and how can we use it to our mutual benefit? *Synergy is the power that a group can manifest that is greater than the combined power of its members.* It means that through the collective consciousness of the group, miracles can be released, goals accomplished, dreams fulfilled that would not have been possible to the individual.

There are several ways you can harness this power in your life, and use it for good purposes.

Read This Book and Do the Exercises

There is a very specific intention behind this book. As you know, this book is created as an instrument of empowerment. It is not simply designed to give you a few ideas, and then leave you to flounder. This book is much like the wind in the sails of a sailboat. Properly trimmed, a sailboat can travel around the world using the air that is free to all. If you remain open the synergy unleashed by this book can continue to propel you to attain your dreams.

The synergy created by this book is really very simple. If you have read this far in the book, then you have an intention to awaken to your full spiritual potential in this world. You truly seek to live as a free spirit, fulfilling the purpose of your life.

There are many other people that have this same intention who are also reading this book. Even if you never meet these people, there is nonetheless a collective consciousness of empowerment that is generated. Out of that mutual desire to awaken totally to your full potential, you unleash a great power that can go before you to prepare the way for a life of great happiness and fulfillment.

The only way you will know the truth of these statements is to test them in your own consciousness. Notice how you feel, see if there is a sense of validity. Remember that in the final analysis *you, and only you* can decide what is true about anything in this life!

Form or Participate In a Dream Group

The simplest thing you can do to work towards greater success in your life is to form a small group of friends that support each other in the attainment of dreams. Generally it is better to have a group that is 10 or less in size. It is important that the other members really want your success and do not feel in competition with you.

This is the group that can give you feedback about your dreams and won't feel threatened as your dreams come true. The whole purpose of a support group is to manifest an energy field of success. Try to meet a minimum of once a month so everyone can check on the progress of the other members.

I have been leading a group such as this for years, and have been amazed what miracles have manifested for the members. New relationships, jobs, guidance when it is needed, all have come forth on a regular basis. Form a group today, start meeting regularly, and you will be surprised by the rapid improvements in your life!

Associate with Positive, Successful People

If you wish to walk the high road in life, giving and receiving the highest available, you must choose other people with a similar desire. Quite simply, birds of a feather flock together! So if you want success, choose a successful flock!

This doesn't mean you have to cast aside friends that you may have had that are less than positive or successful. Honoring friendships is always good. But you should make a conscious effort to cultivate relationships that bring the best out of you as well.

The people that surround us have a tremendous influence on our world view. I remember a friend of mine saying that she was having financial hardship, and that everyone she knew was having trouble. Furthermore, she started saying that things were tough in general, and painted a picture that would suggest that financial hardship was the norm for everyone.

It became obvious to me was that she had surrounded herself with a group of people that were having hard times, and she began to conclude that financial hardship was to be expected. Actually, the town she was living in was having a boom, and there was record prosperity at the time. I told her that she needed to change her environment, start to attend new groups, and be careful about the things she stated casually to her friends.

Soon she reported back that she was doing much better, had a good job. She even met a nice man to whom she later got married. She has a new car, and is doing very well.

Success is contagious!

Stay Active in Your Spiritual Group

There are, of course, many different types of churches, synagogues, and temples. Generally the people that are participating in such groups are making some effort to improve their lives. They are reaching for awakening on some level.

There is great power in coming together to honor God, to pray together, and to seek the highest from life. For many people, this is the most accessible group in which the power of synergy can be unleashed.

If you find that your current affiliation is too negative, and doesn't inspire you, then find a group that does!

Attend Positive Seminars!

In this era, seminars are often used to create the power of synergy. I have taught seminars myself for years, and have watched the power of synergy bring good to the people attending them. It is quite amazing to see how seeds for good that are planted in a seminar will bear fruit– sometimes immediately, and sometimes years later.

Make sure to find a seminar that is consistent with your own values. There are many inspirational speakers traveling the country today, and they often have valuable seminars to attend. Robert Schuller, Mark Victor Hansen, Zig Ziglar, and Sam Keen, are just a few of the people that offer seminars or public speaking engagements. Never miss a chance to put some positive input into your mind!

Summary and Action Plan

1. Open yourself to the vast power of synergy, the power of like minds joining to create great good.

2. People such as Carnegie and Edison used synergy to create great success and bring great good to the world. You can do it too!

3. Associate with positive, successful people whenever possible.

4. Stay Active in a spiritual group that you find supportive. It may be a traditional church, or an informal group of friends. God knows no limits!

Exercise:

Form a dream support group of friends that will meet at least once a month. There doesn't have to be any fixed format or structure, or even size. What is important is that the other members are truly supportive of you, and that you are supportive of them. It is also important that all members are open to the idea of miraculous occurrences, because this creates the energy field out of which miracles are born.

Chapter 9

Live Beyond Competition!

Compete! Compete! Compete! This is the battle cry of the world. There are constant messages from the media that in order to succeed, we must constantly be on the alert for other people who may compete and take away our prosperity, our good. A recent business magazine has this heading on its cover: *Watch your Back! You have more Competitors than you Think!* This is typical of the traditional attitude of success. You are encouraged to see other people as enemies, capable of taking your good from you unless you remain ever vigilant.

Yet there is a way to live in this world free from the constrictions of competition. You can come to know a success, peace and prosperity that goes beyond any need to compete. This is a new way of living in the world. This is the high road, the path to supreme happiness, and complete freedom.

Deep in every soul is a desire to live freely and joyously in the world. We sense inwardly that life was meant to be a joyous, free experience. Yet so often this seems to be an elusive dream, always out of reach. All around us the messages of limitation are constantly being reinforced. Without realizing it we conform ourselves to the limitations of the world rather than awakening to the freedom that is our birthright.

In this chapter you will learn how to live freely, beyond the fears of competition and struggle. Dare to open yourself to the higher vision of your own nature!

No Person Can Take What is Yours

We are normally taught that our good comes from other people. This can come in the form of jobs, relationships, or money. The flip side of that coin is that other people can deprive us of our good. It is this belief system that is the source of all fear and struggle.

If you wish to be free, you must discover who and what you really are. You must begin to comprehend that the very creative power of life resides right within you. You have at your disposal the unlimited power of creation. The universe is unlimited and inexhaustible. As the truth of this begins to soak into your awareness, you will see that each human being is the weaver of his or her own destiny. *No person can take from you that which is yours to possess.*

Once you recognize that you are the source of your own life a tremendous burden will be lifted from your shoulders. No longer will you look at others as potential threats. No longer will the success of others arouse jealousy within you. Instead, you will celebrate each person's evolution.

You will cease coveting what other people have, whether it is a relationship, a job, money, or possessions. You will know that you have exactly what is in your own highest and best interest. As you begin to truly know this as a living reality, a marvelous freedom will enter into your life.

This freedom will release currents of creativity which, in turn, will amplify your own success. You will discover the beauty of working in cooperation with your fellow human beings. You will realize that you can accomplish more through cooperation than competition.

You will look for opportunities to serve your fellow human beings because you will know the great joy that it releases within you. You will also know that as you give, so you will receive. Unexpected joy, prosperity and opportunities will continue to come to you.

All things become possible to the person who is able to empower people. People can sense whether you are *really working for their benefit*, or simply because you wish to *get something from them.*

Wish Competitors Well: As They Prosper, So Will You!

Many people cannot stand the thought of someone who appears to be a competitor doing well, or prospering. They find negative things to say about their competitors, and wish them harm. Little do they know that what we wish upon others is what we really are wishing upon ourselves!

Whenever I see other attorneys who are doing well (or appear to be) I wish them continued success and release them to their own destinies. I realize that their success or failure is not in my hands, but rather arises from their own conduct, their own relationship to the higher self.

When you really begin to trust that your supply is provided by your relationship to the infinite presence of this world, you will see it is an illusion to think others are taking your success.

Let's look at an example in the computer industry. Today many competitors of Microsoft are constantly complaining that the company has become too big, too powerful. Microsoft is the company that introduced the wildly successful "windows" program for the IBM compatible computers. It took them a number of years before the program was accepted in the computer industry, but now it has become the standard. This has made Bill Gates, the founder, one of the wealthiest men in the United States.

Let's look at the actual facts. The success of Microsoft has not only created many millionaires at Microsoft, but it has spawned hugely profitable companies that sell software to work on Windows. It has also stimulated the market for more powerful computers because Windows runs better on this type of computers. It has created a huge stimulant to the entire industry.

What it really comes down to is this: The success of Microsoft has created phenomenal levels of success for many other companies as well. Certainly there are those that have not done as well; but is that the fault of Microsoft, or their own inability to see what the market wants and to supply it?

I would suggest that the competitors of Microsoft would be wise to celebrate the success of the company, instead of constantly attacking it. Once a company is in attack mode it is really on the way out. It is showing its own bankruptcy of new ideas and fresh approaches. Of course, if Microsoft starts attacking others (which many of its competitors think is happening), then it will be planting the seeds of its own failure for the same reasons.

This is what we must all watch out for. When someone new comes along and introduces a new idea, instead of approaching it with fear, we should be happy that new energy, new vitality is coming to the industry. We should look within our own awareness and bring forth our own highest quality of work, and we also will be richly rewarded.

We are Travelers to a Common Goal

We must move to seeing our fellow human beings as fellow travelers moving to a common goal, rather than as potential competitors capable of taking our good from us! As this shift occurs we become less fearful, and our true creativity emerges.

Man Became Rich by Helping People!

As we learn that people are all attempting to do the best they can, and really cannot take our good from us, then a natural desire arises to help out whenever possible. One of the best teachers of this principle in my life is a lawyer/businessman I know. He is the owner of a number of very successful businesses, and also continues to practice law as a hobby more than anything. He is worth many millions.

One day, he and I were working on a case together and I asked him what his secret to success was. He told me that he had two rules that had always worked for him: (1) help people whenever you can; (2) cut the other guy slack if possible.

Over the years he would offer free information and advice to attorneys just starting their practices. He was successful, and had sufficient self-confidence not to regard them as competition.

Additionally, even when an attorney made a mistake on the other side of a case, he wouldn't take advantage of it! He would call up the attorney and warn him of an impending error, or tell him that some document required a response by a certain date. He would always give extensions to the other side, as long they weren't abused.

After doing this for several years, he earned many friends. This brought him in contact with a number of business opportunities that have today made him a multi-millionaire. He still practices law with the same attitude: one of generosity and consideration for the other side.

Consider how different this approach is from the person who feels he must succeed by pushing down or hurting others. Such a person will surely have limited success.

Enlist the Support of People

Your success will, in large part, depend on your ability to gain the goodwill of others. Don't be afraid to ask for assistance from others. Most of the time people will be honored that you wanted their assistance.

Deep within most people is a genuine desire to be wanted, to be needed. When you ask for assistance you actually are contributing to the other person as well.

Million Dollar Case Settled by Enlisting Support

Typically, large lawsuits take considerable time to be resolved. As might be expected, insurance companies would rather defer payment as long as possible. Frequently, the larger the case, the longer the lawsuit takes.

A friend of mine had an experience that proved to me the value of enlisting the support of others rather than engaging in attack. His client had been badly burned in an accident. Right from the beginning he asked the adjuster for the insurance company if there was anything he could give him to make his job of evaluating the case easier. He expressed his willingness to cooperate in every way by giving whatever was requested.

This attitude transformed what could have been an adversarial, conflict-based experience, to one of mutual cooperation—moving towards a mutual goal of case resolution. Within months, the parties all sat down together and by the end of the day had settled the case for over $1,000,000.

What is really amazing about this example is that he *never even had to file a lawsuit!* He simply supplied all the necessary information, including videotapes, and everything the adjuster wanted. The adjuster realized that it was in their mutual best interest to resolve the case without a long delay.

This is a classic case where shifting away from the competition approach to one of mutual cooperation led to excellent results for all parties. The client received his money years earlier than usual, without the stress that is involved in a long lawsuit. The adjuster was served by resolving part of his caseload without lengthy and expensive litigation. Of course, the attorney received payment early, which he liked. In short, everyone walked away better off.

As you learn to move beyond competitive conflict orientation and into the high road of life you will find experiences like this coming to you. Dare to see the people in your world not as enemies, but as travelers toward a mutual goal. It may require a stretch at times, but the results will be well worth it!

Invent Your Own Formula for Success

Too many people try to find success by copying other people. We tend to dress alike, drive similar cars, and conduct our business just like every one else. Then some creative person comes along and does things differently, achieving great success! Yet if we give up the idea of competing with others, and instead look to our own natural creativity, great success will surely follow.

Walt Disney Did It His Own Way!

Walt Disney has always been an inspiring role model to me because he was willing to find his own formula for success. Before he invented Disneyland, amusement parks were considered dirty, dangerous, and certainly poor investments.

But Walt Disney had a different vision. He saw a clean, well-lit place that would embody all American values. It would be a place where a family would feel safe. He persisted in creating his vision even though he had to surmount many difficulties. The rest is history: he invented the most successful amusement park in existence. It has become a place of pilgrimage for tourists the world over.

What few people know is that in his first business ventures Walt Disney became penniless, and success only came as he persisted in the direction of his dreams. If he had tried to create an amusement park like the ones that existed at the time, his name would have never become a household word, and he would have slipped into oblivion.

Don't Worry About the Critics!

What also fascinates me about Walt Disney is that he was willing to implement his own vision, even though he did have his share of critics. Some people said he was a commercial opportunist, creating an amusement supermarket.

He never allowed any of these negative remarks to stop him from pursuing his dream. He was willing to honor his own convictions, and literally millions of people have benefitted.

Have you let critics stop you from pursuing your dreams, the natural prosperity to which you are entitled? Remember that you serve everyone by moving in the direction of your dreams. One prosperous person creates many more. Don't let anyone stop you!

Mahatma Gandhi Practiced Law & Resistance in His Own Way!

Many people are not aware that Gandhi was a successful *lawyer* before getting involved in the Independent India movement. He became very successful by attempting to mediate problems that existed between the Indian merchants who were his clients. He developed the reputation for helping people solve their problems out of court.

Later in his life when he became so active in the resistance movement, he brought a totally new approach. Many of his contemporaries believed they needed to engage in violent resistance to the British. As far as they were concerned, Great Britain was a military empire, and needed to be fought on that level.

Yet Gandhi tried an entirely new and different approach: *peaceful resistance.* He invented that concept, and used it so effectively that he was able to force the most powerful country in the world to grant India independence!

Do you think he would have been as successful if he had just been another violent freedom fighter? I suggest that, if he had, you would have never heard his name, and the struggle for independence would have lasted much longer.

Like Gandhi, you have the ability to follow your own unique path to success. Give up fear of other people and begin to follow your own path. As you do this, you will begin to discover your real purpose for living. You will begin to unlock the natural creativity that is unique to you.

Always remember! You are unique. No other person can make your contribution. Dare to discover who you really are. You won't be disappointed!

Learn to Hold Your Vision, and Ignore Your Competition!

One of the great secrets of success comes when you realize that you have *no competition* whatsoever. All competition is an illusion of your rational mind, which makes it appear that your good comes from other people, places or things. As you begin to understand that your success is born from your own awareness, you will understand that there is a perfect contribution for you to make.

No one else can make the contribution you have to make in life. As you come to realize this, you will understand that no other person can jeopardize or take your success either. This realization will bring great inner peace to you, and will permit you to move steadily in the direction of your dreams.

As you begin to realize that you create your own destiny, you will see how important it is to move your attention away from your competition, and rather to focus on the inspiration within you.

You Will Be Supplied with What You Need to Succeed!

If you are willing to set aside competition, and persist in the direction of your dreams, you will discover what countless others have found: whatever you need to accomplish your dream will be supplied to you.

Answer to Exam Given!

A dramatic example of being supplied what I needed occurred during my first year of law school. I had studied extensively for the exams. However, for some reason I decided to review an obscure study manual the morning of one exam. I happened to look in the very back of the manual and read about a particular problem.

Later that morning I went in to take the exam. Can you imagine my surprise when I saw that the very same question was on the exam! Of course I knew the exact answer, and proceeded to get the highest score the professor had ever given!

As I reflect back on that event it is a classic example of the infinite intelligence moving us forward. I had a strong desire to do well, had dissolved my awareness of competition, and was supplied the very answer that allowed me to excel.

Since that time I have seen this happen time and time again in my life and the lives of those I know. Be open, for answers may be supplied to you in ways that you could never anticipate.

Become accustomed to following the prodding of your intuition. It may be guiding you to an answer that will be profoundly helpful to you at a later time. You are extraordinarily powerful, and will draw to yourself what you need to succeed on every level of life!

Summary and Action Plan

1. There is a high road beyond competition. Your good is waiting for you. No person can take that which is yours.

2. Practice celebrating the success of others. Give up jealousy and envy. They are emotions that can only limit your success.

3. Look for ways to serve people, for as you serve you will prosper.

4. Develop–and honor–your own unique path to success. The greatest success comes not from copying others, but from following your own inner convictions.

5. As you follow your own inner guidance, you will find that answers are supplied to you. Trust and act upon them! When you find your vision, move boldly forward and bring it into reality.

Exercise:

List out the things you enjoy most, and do best and (a) see if you can bring those qualities into the work you are doing now; (b) see how you can evolve your life so that those things become the focus of your life; and (c) practice seeing your "competitors" as simply travelers to the same destination.

Chapter 10

Master Your Work!

This book is dedicated to empowering you to attain your dreams in life. In no area is this more important than your work. *There is a way for you to earn a living, which is joyous, and inspiring to you! Dare to believe this, and move in the direction of your dreams.*

Far too many people spend their days in jobs that are dull and meaningless to them. They live for the weekend, and celebrate Friday's arrival. There is nothing wrong with enjoying the weekend, but we can set up our lives so we enjoy *every day!*

Imagine! Most people will spend the vast majority of their waking hours engaged in one type of work or another to earn a living. Yet many people do not even enjoy this activity. In this chapter, you will be given steps to transform your experience of work, and to have the work of your dreams!

Transform Your Attitude About Work

The first step to having the work of your dreams is to change your attitude about the work you are doing right now. Once you have learned to see the beauty in what you are doing, then you will be free to stay, or move on, out of freedom, rather than compulsion.

The Story of Two Stone Masons

Many years ago there were two workers building a large stone structure. The first worker would go home to his wife and complain about the difficult work. Day in and day out he complained about the injustice of life, and the difficulty of his work.

One day he noticed that one of his coworkers seemed very happy, and yet was doing the very same work. He went and asked him his secret.

The happy man replied that he felt extremely fortunate to be working on this wonderful temple which would be a place to worship God. It would survive the centuries and give great beauty to many generations. He said that he felt honored to have the opportunity to play some small part in this great work of art.

So you see that one man's drudgery was another's art and love. This, of course, is the key to all truly great achievement. We must cease seeing our work as a mundane, meaningless activity, and instead see the beauty and opportunity that it holds.

Whatever your job, there is some way you can contribute to the people around you, and when you do this you will experience a great reward. When you understand that you are immensely important to God, you will begin to see that you can do God's work in whatever job you are currently in!

Imagine living each day as though you were directly serving God, the infinite presence of this universe. Suppose that an angel appeared to you and told you what to do. Wouldn't you feel enormously blessed to have this opportunity? You would feel great joy just knowing you were serving the fulfillment of God's plan.

This is exactly what you are doing, whether you realize it or not. You are critically important to God and the world exactly in the job that you are doing right now! Allow God's blessing to transform your experience of the day and you will live in continual joy.

Learn from the Waitress

I had a personal experience that truly taught me that a job is what we make of it. I used to have lunch at very busy restaurant. Many of the waitresses seemed harried with their jobs.

But there was one waitress who was in her late 50s who always had a great big smile on her face. When she would come over to my table she would put her arm on my shoulder and give everyone a warm welcome. She obviously had a great time playing with and teasing all of her customers. What I noticed is that not only did she enjoy her work immensely, but we also insisted on giving her a large tip every time we ate there.

To me that demonstrates true intelligence on her part. Not only did she turn her job into fun by playing and interacting with her customers, she also dramatically increased her income! No matter what your job is currently, you can do the same thing. Start playing at it!

Complete Your Experience of Work and Move On!

One of the great secrets about work is that as long as you resent it, and are judgmental about it, you tend to be stuck in it! But when you are willing to release all judgment, and all anger towards your work, then opportunities often open up for entirely new possibilities.

The secret of completion is that you must be willing to truly honor the perfection of what you are doing. In other words, you must learn the lesson that the work serves in your life. If you haven't learned the lesson, then you will tend to remain there for much longer. It is really quite simple. When we learn the lesson from something, we are free to move on or stay. The funny thing is that often, when we give up all judgment and resentment towards our work, we often start enjoying it!

When you can really say you are enjoying your work, then at that time you will probably find that you have all sorts of opportunities surrounding you. Dare to start enjoying your work now.

Learn to Serve Through Your Work and You Will Prosper!

Often when we are judging our work, our supervisors, or our clients, we do not attain much success. It is difficult to both condemn, and succeed at the same time. Even though we often don't see it, most judgment is a projection of feelings of inadequacy on our own part.

We project angry thoughts on those that are successful, not realizing it is just a defense mechanism to cover up our jealousy. But as we learn to truly release judgment on those that are successful in our field, then we learn to take our position among their ranks.

This is what happened in my own life. I was very judgmental towards the legal profession (some of you probably would say with good reason). I projected anger and contempt early in my career. As long as I had this attitude I never prospered.

Then a new awareness came to me. I could make a major contribution to the quality of people's lives by bringing my own unique approach to law. I worked to help people resolve their disputes peacefully, and to minimize their time in court. I gave up judgment on other lawyers since I realized they were simply performing their careers in the way they regarded best.

My reputation soon spread and I became financially successful. I began to have tremendous choices in both the kind of work I did, and the way I conducted my business. Although there are certainly things that could be improved in the legal system, I discovered my greatest contribution was to assist people through tough times in their lives with the minimum of stress.

So you can see I found a way to honor my work, and in so doing I prospered. I served my clients, and in so doing I was served with great prosperity and freedom. The same principle applies to every single job. We can always serve people in whatever our role is.

Regardless what you do, you can extend a smile, a peaceful optimistic word. People hunger for optimism and happiness. If you supply it you serve them and God!

Treat Every Day like a Vacation!

One of the great secrets for enjoying and transforming your daily work into great fun is to view it as part of a vacation. Have you ever noticed what you really do on your time off in the name of fun? One day I was sitting on the roof of my vacation home, repairing it from wind damage. I noticed that I was really enjoying what I was doing. The day was beautiful and, it was my choice to do this work.

Suddenly it occurred to me; here I was "playing" at what someone else would call work. If I was getting paid to do this it would seem like work, yet because I was on vacation it seemed like fun.

I had a similar realization while planting some rose bushes. Where I live the ground often is very rocky and hard, so the job is really quite difficult. So there I was breaking my back to plant these flowers and I started thinking about the things we do for fun, and realized that in many cases they are more difficult than our work!

On the highest level, we can actually see our entire human life as a divine vacation, a choice to be here on the planet earth, expressing our creativity. Although most of us don't remember it, in all probability our presence here is a conscious choice. After all, you are one with an infinite presence of intelligence. What makes you think you just happened to arrive on the planet earth?

You probably signed up for an excursion vacation, and are just here having fun! Remember when you go to a movie it isn't any fun if you constantly remember it is a movie. Only when you forget you are in a theater, and become absorbed in the story do you consider it a good movie.

What makes you think life is any different? You forgot who you are, and what your powers are so that you could become fully engrossed in the story you are creating. But now, as you are reading this book, you have decided to create a new story, one with much greater choice and power!

Awaken, and remember who you are! Choose happiness, and master your work. Make a commitment to yourself: *either start enjoying what you are doing, or change what you are doing!*

Is Your Work Right for You?

In this day, living in a free nation, you probably have more opportunity to find the work of your dreams than most people ever have had. You have the good fortune of living in a free society, where you can dream up a new job and start it. If your idea is good, the sky is the only limit that exists on your success.

There are new opportunities being generated every single day. Entirely new technologies are starting up that require new experts, new support products. It takes less capital to start many businesses today than ever before. You can buy a powerful computer and word processor that doubles as a voice mail machine for under $1000 today. The same equipment in 1980 (if you could have found it) would have been vastly more expensive and limited to a few companies.

With the advent of telecommuting, and virtual offices you can start right from your home, with little or no investment. All you need is the idea, and the willingness to get out there and try. The possibilities are unlimited!

Consider these examples of people who changed their careers and moved in the direction of their dreams.

He became Shakespearean Actor

One man I know worked as the manager of a department store. But he found the work was high pressure, and for him held few rewards. What he really loved was Shakespearean acting. So he sought out a company that did Shakespearean performances, and soon had his first role.

He was careful not to give up his primary job at first. Instead he performed in all of his spare time. Then there came a time when his reviews were good enough and the demand was great enough that he could release his department store job.

When I met him, he was working at a summer Shakespeare Festival in Utah. He loved the work he was doing and looked much younger than his age.

His story illustrates what each of us can do. We can begin in our spare time to pursue the activities that we find rewarding. With persistence we can often evolve our lives into a whole new area.

She Started Her Own Craft Business

Another friend worked as a bank teller for many years. Then the bank merged with another bank and her position was eliminated. She had always dreamed of starting a sewing and craft business. She put the word out to friends, and now has more business than she can handle.

She started her Own Magazine

One of the more fascinating cases I have had involved one of my bankruptcy clients. She had over-committed herself and when the economy turned down, she had to declare bankruptcy. But she didn't succumb to self-pity or see herself as a failure.

Instead, she decided to start a new craft magazine. I didn't hear from her for about two years. Then she showed up in my office with amazing news. She had saved over $100,000 and had an enormously successful magazine.

Think of it: from bankruptcy to $100,000 in savings and a successful business in two years. What always amazed me is that she started the magazine with virtually no capital! She simply took advance subscriptions until she had enough money to do her first publication, and from there everything snowballed.

Be a Contrarian Thinker

If you really want to be free in this life, be willing to think of things from a perspective contrary to what most people use. Challenge the basic assumptions about the type of work you do. *The best ideas concerning your current or future work have not yet been thought, or put into practice.* You can be the one to bring them into reality if you want to. You have the ideas within you if you are willing to trust them.

Consider these ideas related to your future work:

Work Smart, Not Hard!

We have all been taught that the secret of success is hard work. But if hard work was really the key to success, then people involved in manual labor would receive the highest pay because that is the hardest work. In truth, success comes to people that work the smartest, not the hardest.

The Easy Way May Be the Right Way!

All technological progress, all wealth, is built on people's ability to make tasks easier to accomplish. For example, the invention of the automobile has created enormous wealth for countless people. And what was the automobile designed to do? It allowed people to get from one place to another faster and easier than by horse.

Or look at the advent of the computer. It makes many tasks far easier than ever before. It used to take a huge amount of time to type and prepare documents. Now, with modern word processors, we can prepare them in a fraction of the time.

We must move beyond the old belief systems that say that earning a living must be hard, or that it is best to choose the difficult road. Why? Intelligence suggests that we should choose the most direct, simplest path to a destination.

This applies just as surely to our livelihood: open yourself to obtaining your financial supply in the most effortless, spontaneous and joyful fashion. Only when you do this will you be honoring your higher self.

Never be afraid to look for an easier way to accomplish what you have to do. It is this desire to simplify that will lead you to great success!

Constantly Improve Whatever You Are Doing!

We have all heard the story of the tortoise and the hare. The hare, although capable of running very fast, failed to follow thorough with finishing the race. On the other hand the tortoise constantly kept moving, and–sure enough–won the race.

This fable is popular because it is so true. No matter what advantage you think other people may have, always remember that if you persist in the direction of your dreams, you can and will attain them. Simple, steady persistence in the direction of your dreams will definitely move you towards success greater than you have ever imagined.

Whatever work you choose to do, remember that (if you look around) there are ways to do it better, more profitably, and to serve your customers more effectively. If you simply set out each day with the goal of finding a better, simpler, more effective way of doing your job, you will eventually be a very prosperous, successful person. Not only that, you will find yourself enjoying your work more every day.

Consider the example of the lowly hamburger, food of the multitudes. There was nothing new about hamburgers when Ray Croc happened to eat at a small restaurant many years ago. They weren't a new invention, but the restaurant was doing an especially quick, clean and efficient job of delivering hamburgers.

Instead of the usual "greasy spoon," the result was an inexpensive hamburger. Ray Croc saw an opportunity, where someone else would have just seen a hamburger. The opportunity consisted simply of taking a very ordinary product and producing it quicker, better, and at a lower price. The result of his willingness to see opportunity can be seen in the thousands of McDonald's restaurants all over the world. Countless fortunes have been made, and hundreds of thousands of employees have work simply because someone did a better job!

Whatever you are doing, there is a better way to do it. Look for it every day; take the extra step to serve your customer or your boss. If you develop this habit, your success will soar, along with your bank account!

Summary and Action Plan

1. Change your attitude about the work you are doing today. You will be surprised how much more enjoyable it will become right away.

2. As you change your attitude you will find your success increasing, and your income growing.

3. Once you have given up working, and started playing, you will find that your spectrum of opportunities will expand. You will have the choice to move to new fields, or stay where you are. Strangely enough, you may realize that you really don't want to change fields after all.

4. Constantly improve what you are doing. Even if you move slowly, you will eventually stand at the top of your field, business or profession.

Exercise:

Get a piece of paper, seclude yourself and honestly consider the answers to these questions:

A. What do you most enjoy doing with your recreational time? What is your favorite pastime?

B. What do you consider yourself good at? Are you a good negotiator, a good salesperson? Are you good with numbers, good with computers? The list goes on and on.

C. What do other people say you are good at?

D. If you were independently wealthy and could do whatever you wanted, what kind of work would you do "just for the fun of it"?

E. What would you have to do to get work in your preferred activities?

F. What action could you take to immediately move yourself in the direction of your dream job? Set a date by which you will take the action.

Chapter 11

You Have All the Time in the World

Time is the god of the 20th century. We worship time by carrying watches with us everywhere. We time everything, and worry about whether we are working and playing fast enough.

But it doesn't have to be this way. You can live in a relaxed, yet stimulating fashion. You can have all the time you want to accomplish your goals and live your life fully. You can actually start playing and having fun with your life.

Imagine for a moment that you were born before clocks were invented. You would have had no clock–no watch–other than the movement of the sun through the sky. You could not have chased time even if you wanted to. Our rushed world is as much a product of our *slavery to the clock* as anything else.

This chapter is an invitation to transform your relationship to time. You can transcend your old belief systems, and discover an abundance of time that you never dreamed possible. People will marvel at how much you accomplish while remaining happy and unrushed.

Einstein Understood that Time Is Flexible and Fluid

If you really want to be free from the burden of time, you must be willing to contemplate the idea that time itself is fluid and changeable. Consider the possibility (no matter how unlikely it may seem) that as an unlimited being, living in an unlimited world you actually have the ability to *recreate time.*

This sounds like a tall order, perhaps bordering on fantasy. After all, the mind reasons, time is fixed and cannot be changed. There are only 24 hours in a day, what more can we do? These are the kinds of thoughts that keep us limited to the dominant belief system about time.

Yet, Einstein and many other scientists have actually proven that time is flexible, fluid-like, and changeable. Our rational minds cannot understand this, but we can intuitively begin to grasp how we can be free from the strictures of time.

Imagine that time actually orients itself around the events you create in your life, rather than the events being within the framework of time. This requires some mental stretching. For example, imagine that your dream is *to start a business.* If you are willing to pursue your dream with faith, not only will you be supplied with the means to accomplish it, you will also be given the time to do so!

Hopi Indians Had No Word for Time!

Before you conclude that these ideas about time are ridiculous, consider that some cultures, such as the Hopi Indians, had no word for the concept of time, and did not view life from the perspective of time. It is difficult for us to even comprehend a culture where there is no word for time, nor any focus on time. They obviously didn't spend their lives rushing around to meet one deadline after another!

The fact that there is a culture that didn't refer to or focus on time should be a reminder to each of us that our concept of time is an invention of our culture. The question is do we like the way we have created it, or is there a better way, one that makes life a more relaxed, spontaneous experience?

Change Your Experience of Time

So what can you do to change your approach to time? How can you create more time by putting these ideas into practice in your own life?

Dare to Slow Down!

We must be willing to slow down, to take time to enjoy the subtle nuances of our lives. Stop and smell the roses. Enjoy the sunsets, and small moments of every day. This is the real point of this chapter. If you want to slow down and enjoy your life more you must take the first step. *You must refuse to let events determine the pace at which you live your life.*

Norman Vincent Peale has said that if you are willing to slow down you will discover God will give you everything you need in perfect timing. He related the story of the day that he was rushing from one meeting to the next, always a little more behind, always a little more tense.

Finally, it dawned on him that he was working himself into a frenzy. He was expected at a dinner and simply told everyone he would be a little late. He stopped, reflected on the idea that God was his source. Once he had fully relaxed then he went down to dinner. He had only missed the soup. No harm came from his delay. From this experience he made the commitment not to rush all the time.

You and I must do the same thing if we want to attain mastery over time.

Give Up Your Attachment to Long, Slow Processes!

After you have slowed down, perhaps the easiest thing that you can do is to open yourself to quicker, simpler paths to your goals. Many times we start thinking that we have to take many steps in preparation for a goal, or that years of effort will be involved. But what if you, as a creative being could open yourself to an answer right now? This would require you to give up your attachment to the process of getting to your goal. You would have to be willing to have it be easier than you thought it would be. Is that okay with you?

Example: Suppose that you want to start your own business. You have heard that you must save up certain amounts of capital; that you must do market research. But in your heart you know that you are ready to begin with your resources exactly as they are. You may be able to proceed immediately and literally save years of time. This book is filled with examples of people who had a hunch for a business, took action and reaped great success. Not one created a business plan, or went by the "book" in creating the business. They followed their instincts, and reaped great success. So can you–much sooner than you think!

Be Open to Unexpected Good Coming to You

As you practice seeing yourself as one with an unlimited source of prosperity, peace and happiness, you will find dreams and goals are fulfilled spontaneously with almost no effort. We are so used to thinking that effort and time must be invested to create an outcome, but in many cases this simply isn't so.

He Created a Motor Home Effortlessly!

Consider the example of Lee. Lee is a good friend of mine who paints houses (among other things). He has chosen to live a very free existence, not encumbering himself with a lot of possessions. One day he saw a beautiful Mercedes Benz Motor home. It had a diesel engine in it, and was in excellent condition, with very low mileage. It ran well, and visually looked great. At the time he was changing his living situation and he realized that if he could get a motor home this would be very helpful to him.

The problem was that he really didn't have any money to his name (he was living on the edge). He went to the owner of the Mercedes and asked him what price he wanted for the motor home. The owner replied, "$10,000, $5,000 or $500, you tell me." Lee jokingly replied he would be willing to buy it for $500, expecting the owner to laugh. Instead the owner said: "Ok, you bought it."

This presented a challenge for him since he didn't have the cash at that time. A little later in the day he mentioned this to a person he had only met one other time, and suddenly the person turned around, and pulled five $100 bills from his pocket and said: "Take this, and buy it!" He couldn't believe his eyes. Suddenly, he was presented with the money to buy the motor home. What is amazing is that the man who gave him the money even told him he didn't have to pay the money back!

Lee came to my office, driving the motor home, and related the whole story to me. The title was good; there were no problems at all with the motor home. In fact, he had to call the Mercedes company, and they told him the current value was about $12,000, and that it would be very easy to sell it at that price.

So you see how God (the universe, whatever name you choose), was able to supply Lee with exactly what he needed with almost no monetary or time investment whatsoever?

We are always being presented with opportunities such as this if we are open to them. The key is remaining open. I have known Lee for years, and he has attended my classes, and has spent considerable time working on awakening to his higher self. Obviously, the work he is doing has paid off!

Re-create the Time in Your Life!

As discussed above, Einstein said that time is fluid. The great masters have said time is an illusion. Why not trust that the real source of time is right within you, and recreate time in your world so you have plenty? I like to experiment with these ideas, as you can see in my Court Experiment described below:

(1) Court Experiment

One day I made a very conscious experiment with time. I was supposed to be in court at 9:00 am. But unfortunately, about an hour before that my chickens escaped (great excuse). I had to spend about 30 minutes searching for them before I got them returned to the pen. Then I left for court knowing I would be there at about 9:30 am, about ½ hour late.

So I tried this experiment. I relaxed while driving to court, and just decided that because I was the master of time, there would be no problem. I arrived at the courthouse, and there was a big sign over the Judge's door: "Court today will be delayed until 9:30 am due to Judge's Meeting." I was amazed. I knew I would be 30 minutes late, and suddenly the court had been rescheduled, that very morning to start 30 minutes late. Because of this change I arrived there exactly on time!

Did my experiment have anything to do with the change? Of course, the rational mind would answer with a resounding "no." Our logical, thinking mind, has great difficulty in contemplating that perhaps it really has such great power. My proposal to you is that we *do* have such unlimited power, if we can begin to assume mastery. But it takes *complete faith, complete assurance.*

Most of us are so imbued and conditioned to think that time is an external power *over* us that we find it very difficult to think we can *recreate it.* But start (in some safe setting) experimenting with your own mastery over time. Start to believe, and practice believing, that *time is unlimited, and you have the power to create it in perfect harmony.* Let this begin to soak into your mind. You will be amazed at the results.

Stop and reflect for a moment. Don't you know some people that seem to have much more time than others, and yet get everything done? Why is it that other people always seem rushed and never get anything done? It is because they are each creating life differently through their own inner power.

(2) A Tale of Two Realtors: One rushed, One Peaceful.

Joanne, a friend of mine, is a realtor. She has been very successful, but somehow she always is out of control. She is always behind, and never can catch up. Her life is a frenzied pattern of action. If you were to ask her why she is so busy, I am sure she would say that is just the way it is. She has a very harried life and frequently seems "stressed out."

Mary, another friend of mine, is also a realtor. Mary seems to have all the time in the world. She has traveled with me on a number of seminars I have taught. She has taken two cruises this year so far. Although she works in this relaxed fashion she always has plenty of money and lives a very good lifestyle.

What is the difference between these two people? Joanne has never realized *her own power* in setting up and ordering her life. She has never realized that time itself can be her servant.

On the other hand, Mary has spent considerable time on evolving and actualizing her awareness. She knows that she is responsible for her life creation, and has refused to let time run her.

If you could see these two lives, you would realize that we have tremendous power to chart our own relationship to time. *Nothing can really force us to rush around other than our own fears, our own doubts.*

A Four-day Work Week, a Three-day Work Week?

Very few people ever challenge the idea that a five-day workweek is normal. Yet that workweek period is purely a cultural agreement. Some societies (such as Korea) regularly work longer, and other societies have no formal workweek. Just as we all have different sleep requirements, so our work patterns are different.

Perhaps you would be better working 3 days on/3 days off, or some other variation on the theme. You can begin to reorder your work schedule if you are self-employed, and experiment with what works best for you.

Several years ago, after one of my seminars I became motivated to change my own schedule. I decided that I would not work on any Monday anymore, barring some emergency. I simply scheduled around the Monday. You know what happened? Nothing. I lost no business. As a matter of fact my income doubled since that time. Now I am experimenting with even more creative schedules.

Even if you are not self-employed you probably have much more control over the time schedule of your work than you think. Many employers are interested in having part-time employees. This gives them flexibility that can be handy, without the expense of full-time employees. Perhaps you could become an independent contractor, offering your services to more than one employer.

The point is that you are creating your relationship to work. Open your mind to far more creative possibilities. You do have the ability to assume the mastery of time in your life.

Summary and Action Plan

1. Slow down, stop and enjoy the subtle nuances of your life. You will pass this way but once. Don't waste the opportunity to find true happiness and joy. After all, what is so important that it justifies giving up your peace of mind, your serenity?

2. Time is fluid and changeable. Dare to trust that you will always have enough time, and you will!

3. Be open to unexpected good coming your way that could save you tremendous amounts of time.

4. Be creative in your approach to your dreams and goals. You may be surprised at how quickly and effortlessly they can come into your life.

Exercise:

Take a sheet of paper and list:

A. What would you start today if you had the time to do it?

B. What are the things that you tell everyone else you would be doing if you had the time?

C. What easy steps could you start today to save time? Example: go to the market and bank less often, stop balancing your checkbook (I can see your reaction now), eat out more often; do things in parallel time (wash the dishes and do the laundry at the same time, not one after another).

D. Practice seeing time as an unlimited substance. Trust that you will be supplied with all you need to fulfill your life purpose comfortably and in a relaxed fashion.

E. How could you spend less time at work (if you want to)?

F. Start doing the things you listed in A and B today and stop using time as an excuse!

Chapter 12

Immunize Your Mind From Negativity

The information you put into your mind is the food that produces the circumstances of your life. If you supply your mind with a diet of positive, inspiring, exciting thoughts, then surely you will reap a wonderful future.

You must also be aware, however, that in this world there is a tremendous variety of information available to your mind. Have you ever considered the vast amount of negative information that comes at us from every direction in today's world?

We are inundated with stories of crime and pollution, of business and personal failure. It is amazing that any person dares leave their home in the morning after watching the news. All of this negativity can create a hypnotic spell of failure and limitation *unless you learn* to *immunize yourself from its effect.*

After all, when we receive an immunization what occurs? We usually develop immunity to the particular bacteria so that it no longer has any effect on our body. Countless lives have been saved due to vaccines for diseases such as polio.

This chapter is designed to give you tools that will allow you to maintain your consciousness in a wonderful, high place, thereby creating the best future for you.

The Law of Cancellation

A very simple, yet effective tool for protecting yourself from unwanted negativity is the law of cancellation. What this means is that if someone says something to you that limits or discourages you, you can simply say quietly to yourself "I cancel that idea."

This way your subconscious mind understands immediately that you don't accept the statement as being true in your world. As an example, if someone tells you that your ideas have no chance for success, or that you will certainly fail, say to yourself "I cancel that thought."

This doesn't mean you should ignore everything you hear. It does mean you should carefully consider what is being said to assess anything you could learn. But after doing this, it is essential you remove any residual negative suggestion that the person has placed on your mind.

There are simply far too many examples of people accomplishing what everyone else thought was impossible. Remember, whenever people make comments to you, they are simply reflecting and projecting their own state of consciousness.

The cancellation system can be used even when you find yourself considering negative outcomes. We all have tendencies to let our minds wander, and sometimes we allow them to wander into negative images. This could relate to any part of your life, your relationships, or your work.

For example, suppose you are driving along and suddenly start wondering what you would do if you were in an accident, imagining an accident. The second you catch yourself imagining or thinking something that is not positive—something that is not what you want to create in your world–immediately stop those thoughts, and state to yourself "cancel that."

When you really start observing your thoughts you will be surprised just how often you engage in negative thinking. It is so easy to slip into images of a failed marriage, a failed business. Without realizing it, we may actually be bringing that reality into our world.

The law of cancellation can be a powerful tool to retrain your mind to think positive, inspiring visions of your future. You can direct the thoughts of your mind, and this will permit you to do so consciously, with purpose. You will be amazed at how effective this is in redirecting your mind into positive futures.

Reprogram your Subconscious with New Core Beliefs

A very effective tool for strengthening your mind is the use of affirmations. If you repeat a series of affirmations on a daily basis you will be providing your mind with powerful food to create the miraculous good to which you are entitled.

Affirmations can be a powerful tool to reprogram your subconscious mind. We all have had years of doubt, both self-generated and from others. If we plant a powerful daily dose of positive thoughts into our mind, it is sure to produce amazing results.

I prefer to use affirmations that represent my core beliefs about life, essential ideas that remind me about how I choose to view life and this world. By repeating them on a daily basis I counteract the barrage of negativity.

I am including here 12 essential core beliefs that I use on a daily basis. Use those that support the awareness you want to create. Also, see the exercise at the end of the chapter for instructions on creating your own affirmations.

1. I feed my mind, spirit and body with powerful, creative, inspired thoughts and ideas on a daily basis. Wonderful results come to me daily in expected and unexpected ways.

2. I remember the power of the spoken word, both on my mind, and the minds of those being spoken to. I use my word powerfully and productively, for joy, happiness, and prosperity for myself and others!

3. Every emotion of happiness, excitement, love, enthusiasm, and divine joy exists within my mind right now. I now have the ability to access these states at will, and consciously decide to live in a supremely joyous, ecstatic and centered state continuously!

4. I surrender all fear to you, God – today and forever. I trust totally in your guidance for all things. I recognize that the opportunity of this life is to trust totally and to transcend fear. I live in ever expanding peace, joy and ecstasy. Wondrous good comes forth now and always.

5. I live more effectively every day. I know everything necessary for a life of great joy, success, divine awakening and satisfaction, now and hereafter. I increase my knowledge about life daily.

6. I confidently follow my convictions and intuition because I realize that to be fully creative and awakened I must give up the fear of being wrong. I also remain open to correction of my ideas as new awareness comes to me.

7. The future (including my own future), holds un-imagined wonders of joy, prosperity, and spiritual fulfillment, greater than my most wonderful dreams.

8. I live in a world of divine abundance, and will now, and in the future be abundantly supplied with money, time, good health, joy, freedom and love.

9. I am free from limiting beliefs, habits, or superstitions about life. I have the discretion to accept the best, and leave the rest.

10. I give the best, and I receive the best in all ways.

11. I am open to wonderful, exciting, creative ideas for all parts of my life, bringing forth new creations of love, harmony and prosperity, for myself and others.

12. I am rich beyond my wildest dreams. I embark on wonderful new adventures every day filled with inexpressible joy. A wealth of money, opportunity, love and happiness has come to me, my loved ones, and friends.

Limit Television, Newspaper, and Movies

There certainly is good programming available on television. The problem is that there is also so much violent, negative programming. Even if you are watching a good program, advertisements will come on showing some act of violence on a different show.

Consider for example that the average child watches 7,000 hours of TV before entering Kindergarten; 11,000 before graduating from high school. By the time a child reaches 7th grade they have seen an average of 8,000 murders, and 100,000 other acts of violence according to a study reported in February 1992, by the American Psychological Association (APA).

Violence on TV does have an effect on people. It has been shown to make children more aggressive: a 30-year study was performed by Leonard Eron, PHD, and chairman of the APA's commission on Violence and Youth. He discovered that the heaviest viewers of TV at age 8 were those later convicted of the more serious crimes, including crimes of violence, and more likely to be violent with their own children.

Unfortunately, this diet of negativity and violence has a tremendous impact on people's outlook on life. They begin to feel that the world is an unsafe, violent place to be, and life begins to fulfill that expectation.

So, what can you do to limit the negative effect of media in your life? This is what I have done in my own life:

Refuse to Watch any Show that Portrays any Act of Violence

View your mind as a sacred trust and do not place any violent, negative images into it. Of course this rule will eliminate a vast amount of entertainment since so much of it is based on violence, but you will find yourself immensely happier if you give it up. At the very least, reduce to a minimum this type of viewing.

Reduce Your TV and Movie Viewing

The simplest way to minimize the impact of media on your mind is simply to reduce or eliminate it. It is incredibly easy to waste countless hours every week watching TV. Consider setting a time limit, or deciding in advance which shows you want to watch. Or you may want to even consider eliminating TV completely for a period of time.

I have experimented with completely giving up broadcast television, and have found it to be surprisingly pleasing. It feels good to be free from the daily barrage of negative information. Instead, if I wanted to watch the TV I would get a video with material that met my own standards, which left me feeling far better.

A positive side effect of reducing or giving up TV is that it will enhance your creativity. TV entertains us by presenting fantasy versions of life, thereby distracting us from our own lives. This tends to sap our creative energies, and fosters the illusion that we are living more creative lives than we really are. *In other words, we accept the TV fantasy in our lives, rather than creating our own fantasies.*

Let me assure you, this life is so fabulous, so unlimited in its potential, that you don't need commercially manufactured fantasies. When you live a truly prosperous, empowered life, your life transcends any fantasy on TV, or the movies. This *is* the magic kingdom after all!

Reduce Your Exposure to the News

Beware of news programs in particular, whether on TV, in newspapers or elsewhere. Certainly news stories can be interesting and valuable. But all too often, the news presents an inherently distorted outlook on the world. The distortion is skewed dramatically towards a bleak outlook on life.

News stories are almost always focused on the small percentage of the world that is completely dysfunctional. There are literally billions of news stories everyday, because there are billions of people. Yet, in all probability all you will hear on the news is stories about the very, very small percentage of people that are involved in some exceptionally *dysfunctional, failing* experience.

You will hear about a cult's fanaticism, but you won't hear about the wonderful works of charity of the countless respectable churches, synagogues, and temples. You will hear about the business failures, but you won't hear about the numerous businesses that are prospering and growing. You will hear about the people who are involved in violence, and degradation, but won't hear about the vastly larger group of people that are living peaceful, productive lives.

The effect of this incredibly distorted view on life is that it distorts the outlook of the viewers. We begin to develop a bleak outlook on life, thinking we are faced with severe, insurmountable problems.

Studies have shown that people who are heavy TV watchers actually see the world as being more violent than it really is. They are more afraid of being involved in some act of violence than non viewers. In fact, it has been shown that such fears are grossly disproportionate to the actual risk.

This negative slant on life can poison your mind, causing you to give up pursuing your dreams out of fear. It boils down to this: if you want to have the best, you have to put the best into your mind! You cannot keep dumping negative, distorted information into your mind and expect to prosper and succeed.

If you are unwilling to give up news completely, try to find some journal that you feel is somewhat balanced, and get your information from that source. Most importantly, start making your own news. Become so successful that people start wanting to write stories about you!

Summary and Action Plan

1. Your mind is a sacred trust. The mental food you put into your mind will have a tremendous effect on the quality of life you experience.

2. Use the law of cancellation to protect yourself from negative ideas, whether they originate in your mind or from words spoken by others. Silently cancel any thought that you do not want to accept as true in your world.

3. Minimize the input of negative media. Reduce your watching of violent entertainment, and minimize viewing the news media. If you watch a lot of TV or movies, you can easily be hypnotized into a much more pessimistic and limited world view. Utilize videos in choosing positive entertainment, and be selective about what you put into your mind.

Exercise:

Use positive affirmations to install new core beliefs in your subconscious mind. Write down at least 10-12 statements of inspirational ideas. Feel free to use the statements included in this chapter, or rewrite them so they are comfortable to you. The language should be something that you find simple and inspiring. Try to repeat some or all of your affirmations on a daily basis. You will be surprised how uplifted you will be before you are done!

Chapter 13

See and Expect Only Good!

You have probably heard many times that it is important to be positive in your outlook on life. But if you really want to attain your dreams *you must go beyond merely being positive*. You must truly trust that good–and only good–can come into your world. You must be willing to leave behind your belief in bad things.

This means that no matter what happens in your life, you must step back and say to yourself that it holds only good for you. Even if you cannot see what the good is at the moment you must trust that good will come to you. Sometimes the good comes immediately; other times it may be years off. But if you are willing to truly trust, and place your faith in God, in the very goodness of life, then you will surely reap a good result!

The reason for adopting this state of mind is very simple: *Within you lies a power greater than anything you can ever encounter in this world!* This means that if you expect only good, and refuse to surrender to negative thinking, God can turn any defeat into victory.

Your first reaction to this idea probably is something like this: "I can't give up seeing bad things because bad really happens in the world. If I give up seeing what is wrong, it will never be corrected. Besides, I need to be aware so that I won't be hurt by life. To think that only good happens is naive."

Yet in fact, exactly the opposite is true. If you see things as bad in your world, you will actually "create" them that way. You will put a negative charge on the event or circumstance– which virtually assures that negative outcomes will occur. It is actually true that you cannot afford the luxury of a negative thought.

I am going to give two examples below that show just how this principle can work to produce great results for you:

Earthquake Produces Unusual Benefit!

In January 1994, I got a call from my Dad at about 5:45 am telling me that there had been a very severe earthquake in Los Angeles. He said that his house was in shambles and glass was everywhere. It was the worst earthquake he had experienced in 40 years of living in Los Angeles. Actually, we were lucky he was able to get through to me, because within 10 minutes after that the phone lines were cut off.

This is an event that normally would appear to be negative. He suffered a loss of many thousands of dollars, both in his home and his office. But he has been practicing these principles of positive thinking also. Listen to what happened, for it is quite amazing.

Several months of cleanup had passed, when one day a FEMA (Federal Emergency) employee came out to his house to check out the condition of his house. When the doorbell rang he looked out and there was an attractive woman. After she was finished inspecting the house, my father got inspired and decided to ask her for a date!

She accepted and an exciting romance ensued. A couple of years later they were married. This began an exciting life together, including world travel and romance for both of them.

Now I ask you, was the earthquake a negative or positive event for my father? Obviously, it brought him a lot of happiness in the form of a new relationship. Incidentally, it also led to a completely remodeled house, which was also positive.

The point and lesson is simple: be willing to look for good in all things. Be fanatical about it. If you do this, then you will open up the possibility for truly miraculous things to come into your life–maybe even a new relationship!

Jaguar Rear-ended!

It takes practice to truly expect good under all circumstances. A test that came into my life involved my classic Jaguar XKE automobile. I had spent thousands of dollars restoring it, and it had spent over a year in the shop for various restoration projects.

Finally, the day came for me to pick up the car. It was beautiful, probably even better than when it was new. I got in the car and headed for home. Near my home I pulled off the freeway and came to a stop in a line of traffic. Suddenly I heard a large thumping sound, screeching tires, and the rear of my car was hit!

It was very gentle: so gentle, in fact, I wasn't even sure what had happened. The second this happened, *I paused mentally and said "thank you God, I know good will come of this."* Then I jumped out of the car.

What I saw amazed me. *There was a car that had rolled over.* Immediately behind me there was a large truck turned sideways. I went over to the driver and asked what had happened. He said he had been sitting there behind me, looking at my car, when suddenly he felt *"prompted"* to look in his review mirror.

He saw a car careening towards him, giving no appearance of slowing down. He put his foot on the brake as hard as he could, braced himself and was violently rear-ended. As his truck spun in a circle it hit my taillight, which was the impact I felt.

Suddenly, I realized what a tremendous blessing had occurred in my life. If that large truck had not been between the runaway vehicle and me I almost certainly would have been killed, because of the small size of my car. His large truck was damaged severely, and was spun in a circle. So, truly I was blessed far more than I could even have imagined.

Additionally, I gave my attorney card to the driver of the truck, and he ended up retaining me for injuries sustained in the accident. I ended up making enough from that one case to pay for all the restoration work that had been done on my car! What could have been a terrible tragedy was turned into a wonderful gift.

Can you see how the process works? The event occurred, I immediately proclaimed it as good, saw it as good, and expected good from it. Consequently, as I expected, only good came from it! By the way, that client ended up referring other clients to me, and it led to a number of different cases over the years.

Practice "Miracle-Readiness" to Create Good

In addition to seeing only good, it is critical to expect and accept miraculous good into your life. The idea of expecting miracles has become quite common, but few people really develop a mentality of miracle-readiness.

The secret is to learn to expect at every moment, every day, that miraculous good can come to you beyond all rational comprehension. This can mean everything from unexpected business, to new relationships, to windfalls of any kind. *If you want to really live a miraculous magical life, then you must take the responsibility for cultivating this awareness in your life.*

Every day when you get up in the morning start thinking about all the incredible, wonderful things that could happen to you in the day. Start thinking about how lucky you are to live in a miraculous world that is free from limits. As you do this you will find yourself getting excited about the possibilities that surround you. As you develop excitement, you will be triggering your inner self, which is the key to creating miracles in your world.

She Created Tickets for Play!

Miracles really do happen all the time. The problem is that we so often take them for granted. Consider this example that just occurred in my own family:

My wife woke up Wednesday morning and said she would like to go to a certain outdoor play. We had not been to one of these for over a year. We called the theater and were informed that all tickets were sold out.

Within two hours we received a call from my wife's father. He called to ask her whether she wanted *tickets to the very play she wanted to see, for the same night!* It turns out someone in his office had planned to use the tickets but had a conflict, and then asked him whether he wanted them. He immediately thought of calling my wife, and hence we had our tickets, free of charge!

Stop and reflect! Was this just coincidence? She had not thought of attending this play until that very morning. She had not mentioned anything to her father. But within two hours after the time that she expressed a desire to go, the tickets were made available to her–even though the play was sold out!

This is what is meant by a state of "miracle-readiness." Miracles can come to be an expected and welcome part of your life. The secret is to be honest when miraculous events occur in your life. Don't simply cast them aside as coincidences. Recognize them for what they are: creations born of your consciousness. This way you will come to truly trust in the continuous flow of miracles into your world!

Summary and Action Plan

1. If you want to walk the high road and know a life of outstanding happiness, you must be willing to see good in all things. In this way, you take responsibility for creating good from every circumstance that enters your life.

2. No matter how unlikely it may seem, every event has the capacity to bring you special good. But you cannot take a wait and see attitude. You must take charge of your mind, and know that only good is there for you.

3. At every moment you must be in a state of miracle readiness; completely open and receptive to miraculous, totally improbable events occurring in your life. As your mind becomes saturated with this expectation, you will magnetize all manner of wonderful things into your world!

Exercise:

A. When you wake up in the morning, declare: "I am open to finding all of the wonderful miracles in this day." At the end of the day consider the wonderful things that have happened and go over them in your mind. This way you will begin to see how many miracles really are coming to your life each and every day.

B. Practice viewing every circumstance in your life as holding miraculous potential for good, no matter how far removed it may seem to be. Make a list of the areas of your life that you currently find difficult, or challenging. Then bless each and every one of these conditions and accept that they are transformed through the miracle working power of life into amazing good.

C. If you hear about some negative occurrence or event in your town or city, ask that the circumstances be blessed, and trust that somehow the event will lead to greater good, sooner or later.

Chapter 14

The Two Most Important Words

There are two words that will have more impact on your life than any others in the English language! They affect you on a daily basis. The way you respond to them, the habits you develop for dealing with them will set the very course of your life. What are these words? Yes and No. The two words we learn first in life as children. These have tremendous emotional power over our subconscious minds, and you can learn to harness them to your enormous benefit.

Develop the "Yes" Habit!

"Yes" is an extraordinarily powerful word. It can open doors and take you to entirely new levels of success. If you want to attain greatness in your life, it is very helpful to develop the "yes" habit. This means that you habitually say yes to opportunities that are presented to you, before allowing your doubting mind to get involved.

The whole secret behind the "yes habit" is that you develop an automatic habit of responding affirmatively to opportunity. We all have a tremendous tendency to avoid new experiences. We may feel challenged, or worried about our ability to succeed. By getting in the habit of saying yes immediately, we overcome our natural inertia.

She Said Yes, and Started a New Career

A good friend of mine saw her whole life change by saying yes to an opportunity. She was temporarily unemployed. A mutual friend asked her whether she could come in and help out with secretarial work at a pool company.

At first she thought of herself as unqualified for the position. Then she thought there was nothing to lose since it was only a temporary position. Well, the temporary job turned into a long term job, and guess what happened? A few years ago, the owner decided that he wanted to sell out and she bought the business! She now is the owner of an extremely successful pool company, installing pools in many of the fine homes of her town.

Her entire livelihood today arose because she took a chance and said yes. Had she allowed her doubts to overcome her, she would never have attained the financial and professional success that she now has.

If you are committed to preparing yourself for greatness get in the habit of saying yes–to life to opportunity, to new experiences. Your life will soar to heights you never imagined.

Never Let "NO" Stop You!

You *will* attain great success in life. You will learn to master your mind, your thoughts, and create the future you always dreamed of. One of the secrets you must learn to master is how to overcome any "no" that appears in your path.

We are confronted with many "no's" along the way in our life. When we were children "no' was probably the first word we were taught. In fact "no" is the one word that is almost exactly the same in many languages! Not only that, but often we were punished if we dared to proceed after this word was spoken.

Think about it as the strange riddle of this life: as a child your very survival and well being depended on your willingness to obey the word "no." It made your parents happy, and probably did protect you in many cases. In school your obedience to "no" brought you praise from the teacher.

As an adult, as a fully awakened being, your very survival, success and fulfillment requires you to go beyond the word "no," to transform it into yes, an affirmation of life. No great accomplishment, no great spiritual attainment has ever occurred if a person was willing to accept the appearance of "no."

You must, therefore, be willing to overcome this tremendous programming you have received to stop when you hear "no." You were born to be a human being, an empowered spiritual being. You will never be happy unless you learn to think for yourself. You must learn to have the power to transcend, and transform "no" into yes.

It is axiomatic that the first step towards your dream will be met by a resounding "no." At that moment, you will have to decide whether you will persist in the direction of your dreams, or give up, thinking that all of the doubters were right all along. That will be your test, God's method of seeing whether you are really ready to manifest the creation. Only if you move steadfastly forward beyond that "no" will your dream begin to become true.

He Became Best-Selling Author by Overcoming No!

Consider John Grisham, the author of the best selling novels, *The Firm, The Rainmaker,* and others, a number of which have been made into movies. When he finished his first book, only a few years ago, and submitted it to a publisher, he was turned down! He was told "no, we don't want your work."

He actually had to present his book to 16 different agents before one finally accepted him. It then took his agent a year and 26 submissions to sell his book. That represents 42 no's that had to be overcome to get his book into print. Now he receives a small fortune for his books, and they are made into movies. But this would never have happened if he had allowed himself to become discouraged.

What is fascinating about John Grisham is that he had no background for writing. He actually got a "D" in his freshman English class! His goal was to be a tax lawyer. Now he is a richly successful writer.

Somehow he had the ability to retain his inner confidence in the quality of his work, and this confidence carried him beyond the many rejections he received. You can do the same thing! You can overcome the "no's" in your life if you are just willing to persist until they become "yes's."

There is Always A Way to Your Goal!

The secret of overcoming the rejections you will receive is to be aware that there is always a way to get to your goal. You can always find a crack in the wall, and find your way through. You must know that from a deep inner conviction.

Consider every "no" to be simply a step on the way to your destination. Never see it as a reflection on your abilities, or nature. Just because someone else doesn't see your genius isn't any reason for you to give up your dream!

You can accomplish your goal and your dream, if you are just willing to persist, and not let anyone talk you out of it. That is your challenge, and you can do it!

He Became Successful Business Man by Overcoming No

Did you know that Colonel Sanders did not even begin his Kentucky Fried Chicken business until he was 65 years old! Imagine, most people are thinking only of retirement, and he was off and starting a new business.

He traveled around in his old station wagon speaking with one restaurant owner after another trying to sell his chicken recipe. He was turned down over and over again. Can you guess how many times he was turned down? 50, 100, 200? He was actually turned down over *1,000* times before he found a business to work with.

Would you have been able to overcome 1,000 "no's?" Where would you have stopped?

If you want success in this life you have to be able to overcome the word "no." Once you have learned not to be intimidated by it, you will become vastly more successful, whether in business or in personal affairs.

Summary and Action Plan:

1. Develop the Yes Habit. Routinely respond affirmatively if someone gives you a new opportunity to expand your horizons. You will set a chain of activity in motion that you could never anticipate.

2. Learn to overcome No! This is one of the most important skills to develop. All successful people learn not to be put off by "no." They understand that no is just a step in the process towards complete success!

3. Remember that there is nothing embarrassing about being turned down, or told no. Most of the successful people you know or have heard of have had to overcome many no's to get where they are. Consider "no" a compliment indicating you are on the right path!

Exercise:

A. Make a list of 5 activities or projects you have not done because you are afraid of rejection. List the consequences if you tried and failed. If the consequences are acceptable (for example you might not want to gamble your entire life savings), then choose one, set a date, and move ahead. Repeat this until you have moved down the list of activities that you desire to accomplish.

B. Practice asking for discounts even at stores where you don't think they are available. It is a good way to keep your fear of "no" from becoming too strong. You would be surprised at the number of places that have given me a discount or service that I would not have expected simply because I asked.

Chapter 15

Your Divine Connection: The Secret of Empowerment

You have chosen to live in this world as an awakened being, to walk the high road of spiritual freedom. In a sense this entire book is about nothing other than your relationship to God. No matter how successful we become in this life, how many dreams we have fulfilled, usually there comes a point when we realize there is something more to this life experience. We begin to inwardly sense that our lives fit into a greater and grander pattern than we ever imagined.

What begins as quiet intuition of something greater than our individual life gradually becomes an overwhelming conviction and passion. With this conviction comes a hunger to know the great presence of God that has been the inspiration of all religions.

This is the beginning of the spiritual journey, which in many ways is the most exciting, most fabulous dream of all. We begin to encounter the unlimited possibilities of God, the supreme joy that is possible in a human life.

If we wish to find this supreme joy we must learn to live in faith, literally learning to create our reality from moment to moment. We must be willing to step forward with conviction and power, vanquishing the clouds of doubt from our minds.

Spiritual Growth is Like Riding a Bicycle

Spiritual growth is much like learning to ride a bicycle. Think back to the time that you learned to ride. At first you used training wheels. The bicycle was secure with its wheels in place, but you really couldn't go very fast or far. Finally there came a day when you were no longer satisfied to ride along with the security of the wheels in place; you wanted to accomplish greater things.

So, you took off the wheels. Maybe your mother or father stood there by you, trying to assist your transition. As you began to develop speed there came a frightening realization: you could fall and hurt yourself if you made a mistake. You suddenly found yourself at the crux of a decision; would you push harder on the pedals and trust that you could control your speeding bicycle, or would you slow down and return to the familiarity of your training wheels?

At some point, maybe after trying many times, you found the courage to speed forward on your own. You found your bike wobbling, but somehow in the release of it all, you were doing it! You were really riding the bicycle. Wobbly at first, but with remarkable quickness, you developed speed and control. You walked through your fears and moved to a whole new skill level. The exhilaration was phenomenal. You did it!

This is exactly what you must do your entire life if you wish to walk on the spiritual path. At first it is challenging to walk forward in faith. You have to trust in your higher self, when your rational mind wants to go back to the security of the training wheels of logical thinking.

You know inwardly that there is a universe of freedom just waiting for you, but you are scared. What if you are wrong? What if your faith is misplaced?

Then there comes a glorious moment, a time when you decide to transcend your fears, to quell the screams of the rational mind and to boldly go forward in faith. You stop listening to your own doubts or the doubts of others. You surge forward in faith. You are exhilarated as you realize that you are free, that you are flying!

Just like the bicycle, your initial spiritual flight may be a bit wobbly. You may even have a few mishaps. This is the critical point on the spiritual path. When you encounter these mishaps, will you stop trying to ride the bicycle? Will you decide it was all a pipe dream, and foolish to have believed?

If you give up your faith at this point, you will return to the world of the earth bound, those who are surrounded and defeated by the appearances of the material world. But if you persist in your faith, the very universe will open at your feet. You will discover that you were free all along.

Once you are free you will realize that the very gift of power has always resided in your own consciousness, waiting for you to develop the wisdom to learn how to use it. For it is surely true that you will awaken to power in exact proportion to your self-trust. If you do not trust yourself, you will never allow yourself to really contemplate and exercise your true power. You will persist in believing in yourself as limited and small.

Open Yourself to the Infusion of Divine Intelligence!

As you totally and completely open yourself to infusion from the presence of God, you then become exalted in every way. Your life becomes blessed, your world becomes a place of wondrous good fortune. To others you appear lucky, but in your heart you know that everything that is yours has come from the benevolence of the wonderful presence of God.

You begin to realize that the goodness that comes to you comes not from any particular merit or action, but rather from your willingness to accept the unbounded love of God. This requires you to set aside your own opinion of self and allow it to be replaced by the ever-expanding love of God.

You allow the blessings of Goodness, of God to flow in and around your life–not only to you, but to the others in your world as well. In this way you truly become a blessing and a servant of God.

Great Joy Will Come to You!

As you accept the infusion of divine love into your life, you will no longer just be an individual clamoring for things and possessions, you will have become a light, an instrumentality of the presence of goodness in this universe. Your life will become ennobled, uplifted and exalted. You will sleep in joy, you will wake in joy, taking pleasure in all the simple beauties of life.

You will realize that your spiritual path has taken you to the point that this world, which once appeared mundane and difficult, has become a place of great joy, peace and happiness. You will be serving both God and man, and thus live a life of great fulfillment.

Find Your Own Path to God!

There are many great religions in this world, and countless sincere followers. Each of these traditions has contributed much to the world, to the lives of believers. If you find yourself drawn to a particular religion or path that may be God's way of awakening and teaching you what you need to know.

On other hand, you may find that no religion fully encompasses your inner experience of God. I suggest to you that we all have a unique path of awakening to the higher presence in life. This is the true high road, the road that asks you to honor your own self, your own experience, and your own expression of reality.

Every great spiritual teacher was willing to follow his or her inner prompting. We would never have heard of Jesus if he had simply lived the life of a good rabbi. Instead he followed his own inner convictions and has uplifted countless millions of lives. I challenge you to do as Jesus asked and go out and do greater things than he did!

The Gift of Empowerment!

Perhaps the greatest mystery on the spiritual path is the opportunity of empowerment. As I have said a number of times, this book is designed to be a transformational tool in your life, an actual empowerment in your spiritual sails to guide you to a higher level of existence.

This brings me to one of the great paradoxes of the spiritual path. Although you must make your own connection to the infinite, (and make your own decisions), nonetheless spiritual empowerment from another who has experienced divine freedom can be an enormous assistance.

You see, there is an experience of the infinite that goes beyond any words. An experience of love, of transcendence, of joy that is all pervasive. No amount of words can ever convey this experience, any more than I could describe to you how chocolate tastes. The only way you will ever know chocolate is to taste it yourself. Then you, too, will have the experience.

This is where empowerment comes in. Although words themselves cannot convey the experience of the absolute, the energy field behind the words can be transferred to you! This is why at various points in this book you may feel a sense of happiness and peace, because you will experience the gift of grace that has inspired this book.

Empowerment can actually remove obstacles from your path, and open the doors for the opportunity that God has for you. Empowerment is the assistance of one divine being to another.

Empowerment is like taking one candle and lighting another candle. Once the new candle is lit, it burns its own light.

In short, you and I are communing on a divine level, sharing a mutual experience of the infinite.

The Power of Prayer

This chapter would not be complete without mention of the vast, empowering quality of prayer in your life. Prayer is one of those mysteries for which there is no rational explanation. Someone once asked a master whether prayer was really necessary to one who knew his unity with God. The master answered, of course you should pray, because prayer works! No one knows how or why prayer works but it does. Test it out in the laboratory of your own experience.

Prayer is your great asset, your great gift. It is your lifeline to the infinite, your connection to the absolute. It is your power switch to the unbounded powers of the Higher Self. Of all the things I teach my children, the one that I most want to share with them is the great secret of prayer. If a person knows how to pray, that person will live a happy life. It is the one resource that can never be taken from you, and from which you can draw limitless good into your life.

Pray on a daily basis and you will find yourself filled with radiance and vigor. The form that you pray and the words that you use are not important. What is important is that you make a conscious, vocal (preferably) prayer to God. Your conscious mind may wonder what good such a prayer will do, but prayer can be the activity of spirit within your own consciousness.

Let us assume that you have great power as a divine being on this planet earth. Assume that some event or circumstance occurs in your life and you wish it to turn out in a more positive way. By praying you can utilize this vast power to influence and transform the event.

In other words, the power of God will transmit through you in your part of the universe. You are then acting as the presence of God in that circumstance or condition. Your prayer then becomes a positive divine use of the power given to you. You become part of the solution, rather than part of the problem.

Take everything to God in prayer. Ask God for guidance on things large and small. It is God's good pleasure to take the burdens from your shoulders, but you must be willing to give them over. God will not do what you will not permit! We have freedom of choice; otherwise we would simply be robots carrying out the commands of others.

Every night before you go to bed surrender each and every occurrence of the day to God, and ask that God bring forth the right action. Forgive yourself and everyone else, and get a good night's sleep. Start the next day with a prayer, and ask that you be guided from moment to moment by the Divine Presence that can make the crooked road straight. Ask for it all; you do no favor in asking for less!

Pray and be happy!

Summary and Action Plan

1. Open yourself to the infusion of Divine Awareness into every part of your life.

2. Be willing to trust, and develop faith that you will be supplied at every moment with exactly what you need for your future, spiritually, emotionally and physically.

3. Remember how exciting it was to ride your bicycle the first time. Soon you will be spiritually flying, creating miracles and joy greater than you ever imagined.

4. Follow your own path spiritually. Be willing to honor your own instincts. You–and only you–can decide what is right for you life!

5. Accept the gift of empowerment that this book offers to you. Let it be a wind in your sail, removing obstacles large and small, and guiding you into a future of great joy, peace and prosperity.

Exercise:

A. Pray regularly, peacefully, happily. Prayer is your connection to the absolute. It is your way to plug into divine energy. Do it and your health and happiness will be radiant.

B. Pray for the success and happiness of everyone in your world.

C. Pray for your enemies (if you feel you have any) as well as your friends.

D. Pray knowing that you are a conduit for power greater than you could ever imagine.

E. Pray for 30 days, for 5 minutes in the morning and the evening and notice how your life changes for the better.

Chapter 16

Give Up Worry and Stress Forever!

You can live free from worry and stress! You can know prosperity and peace greater than you ever imagined. You can break the patterns of worry, anxiety, and upset if you really want to! But you must be committed. You will have to change the habits of a lifetime.

Worry is Worthless!

So, how do you give up worry? First you must realize that *worry does no good for you!* Did you know that 95% of what we worry about never comes to pass? The remaining things usually are so minor that we can easily handle them as they arise in our lives.

Most Important Things Can't Be Planned

Second, your worry does no good because most of the major events of your life *could not be planned anyway!* Stop and reflect on your own life. Think about the major events of your life–your significant relationships, your jobs, even where you are living. Now stop and reflect whether you could have really planned most of those events. Most of the time you will see that you could *not* have planned these events.

Met Wife in Totally Unforeseen Circumstances!

An example from my own life, I met my wife when a date I had didn't work out, and I went to a party. My wife happened to be at the party with a friend. They had just stopped by the party for few minutes on the way to another destination.

If I had not arrived just when I did, I would have never met my wife, never had the children I now have. In short, my life would have been completely different. *Yet I could not have planned to meet her–it was out of my control (at least of my conscious mind)!*

This is the great freeing realization. The most important things in your life, (as well as the very minor things) are essentially beyond your ability to plan. We simply do not have the information available to us at the moment we are making decisions to make truly informed decisions.

When you realize this, a great burden will lift off your shoulders. You will see that worry is absolutely unnecessary. Our lives are part of a great flow that is essentially beyond the conscious mind. So why don't you just stop and enjoy the flow of your own life. Worrying won't do a bit of good!

Give Up Worry as an Experiment and Watch the Results!

As an experiment, start today, and simply give up every moment of worry that comes into your mind. Continue for one month. If you start to worry about anything–large or small–simply give up the thought and decide to relax instead. Give yourself a mental vacation for one month. Then, at the end of the month, examine your life. You will be amazed to see that things are working better than they ever have before.

Re-train Your Mind to Live Free of Worry and Stress

In order to give up stress and worry we often have to re-train our thinking process. Often the stress we experience is a deeply ingrained thinking pattern that requires subconscious reprogramming to change.

College Admission Test Teaches Stress Lesson

When I was in college, taking the Law School Admission Test (LSAT), I learned an invaluable method of overcoming stress that has helped me, (and countless others as well) since that time.

The LSAT is an exam designed to assess a student's likelihood of success in law school. The exam score can make a critical difference in the school you get to attend and your career future. It is timed, and often can be a high-pressure experience.

When I took the exam the first time, I was not psychologically prepared. As I sat looking at the questions, I suddenly had a classic case of "test panic." I started thinking of how important it was to my career, and my mind literally blanked out. Needless to say, my score was not great.

I had to take the exam again, but was concerned that the same fears would arise leading to the same poor results. I went to a school counselor and he gave me a system that has revolutionized my approach to examinations–or literally any stress-producing event.

The A/B Stress Elimination Technique

The system I learned was extremely simple and extraordinarily effective. You can use it in your life to dissolve the stress associated with any event. In order to do this effectively, you will need about 15 minutes, and should have a private place where you can sit and relax. Here are the steps involved:

Step 1, Imagine a Relaxing Scene

The first thing you need to do is remember a time somewhere in your past that you were extremely relaxed and peaceful. Or if you can't think of an actual time, then make one up. Let's imagine you have chosen a time you were at the beach.

It is very important to the success of the technique that you vividly imagine the scene in a total sensory fashion. Hear the waves crashing down on the beach. Smell the fresh salty ocean air. Feel the sand between your toes. See the beautiful blue water with white caps, and frothy waves breaking. If there are other people there with you, see yourself talking with them, or just being with them.

As you imagine this relaxed beautiful scene (what I refer to as Scene A), you will find that you become very relaxed and serene. You will feel good on a very deep inner level. If anything was bothering you before you started visualizing, it will fade as you relax your mind and body. It is important that you take about 5 minutes in this first step, becoming very peaceful.

Step 2, Imagine a Scene that Causes Stress For You

This step is critical to the success of this technique. Choose any experience, any event that may cause you stress. It could be anticipation of an examination, a public speech, or a work environment that is unpleasant to you.

Let's assume you wish to eliminate the stress from an upcoming examination. Again, you must get a vivid picture of yourself in the exam setting. What I would usually do is go to the room where I would be taking the exam so I really knew what to expect. I would get the full experience of the room, including its smell and sounds.

Then, after you have spent approximately 5 minutes imagining your relaxing Scene A, (the beach scene), start visualizing the stress removal scene, Scene B. For an exam, start imagining that you are walking up to the exam room. See yourself walking into the room, sitting down. Look around, in your mind, at the people around you in the room. Look down at the test that is being handed out to everyone. Now open the test and look at the first page, usually a set of instructions.

At this point in the visualization process, any stress that you have associated with the scene will begin to surface. You will begin to feel your body tighten up. There is a good chance you won't want to continue visualizing the scene. You would rather avoid it in your mind. *This is excellent, it means you have really tapped into your subconscious programming regarding the particular event.*

Step 3, Return to the Relaxing Scene A

Once you have really begun to experience the moods, the stress or anxiety associated with Scene B, and have spent about 5 minutes doing so, then return to Scene A in your mind. You will find an *immediate* sense of relief. All of a sudden you will find your breathing more relaxed, and your body 'letting go' of stress.

Enjoy your relaxing scene to the fullest. Allow all the residual feelings of tension to disappear. Take up to 5 minutes doing this.

Step 4, Rotate Between Scene A and B until Stress Dissolves

Once you are relaxed, slowly move back into your Scene B (the exam in our example). This time you will notice that you are not quite so tense. Try to just observe the exam, but without the tension that you had previously. Keep remaining with Scene B until you have fully re-experienced it, including any remaining tension.

Then return again to your relaxing scene. Keep rotating back and forth until you can encounter the Scene B without any stress. What will *amaze you* is that the stress you associated with it will literally dissolve. What you have done is associate in your subconscious mind a new response pattern, the response of being relaxed and at peace.

Step 5, Repeat several times a week for minimum of several weeks

I have taught this technique to people taking bar exams, or facing other stressful events. In every case where people 1) actually took the time to do this several times a week, 2) invested 10-15 minutes per time; 3) preferably for several weeks in advance of the event, there have been excellent results.

Woman Gets "A" on College Exam Using Technique

A college student took one of my seminars where this relaxation technique was taught. She had been scoring poorly on her exams. She had become stressed out and upset. She decided that she would try this technique. Imagine my delight when she reported back several weeks later that she had received an A on her next college exam. She was thrilled with the results.

Woman Passed the Bar Exam After Failing Previously

Another woman had taken the bar exam two times previously, and (unfortunately) had failed both times. You can imagine the stress that she was experiencing. After having failed twice, she had a tremendous build up of anxiety and fear.

I made a special tape for her, guiding her through this visualization process. She listened to it every day in the weeks preceding the examination. She took the exam and passed with flying colors! To this day she gives credit to that technique.

Eliminate Reality Shock When Returning from Vacation!

Many times I have taught seminars at beautiful vacation resorts. One of the problems most people have when they are on a wonderful vacation is the fear and in some cases dread of returning to their daily lives. They have touched an empowered, enlivened experience of life and don't want to return to the world they had left.

This same stress reduction technique can be used to take back with you the wonderful feelings of liberation and excitement that you had on your vacation. In order to do this simply take 5 minutes a day when you are on the vacation and visualize yourself back in your home environment. If any feelings of stress or fear arise, let go of the home picture and return to being on vacation.

If you do this on a daily basis, you will find you have already returned home in your mind, and have literally re-programmed your response. There will be no upset or frustration when you get home. *Instead you will have programmed in your vacation mood and will have brought it home with you!*

You may think that it couldn't be that easy. But many people have used this technique for a number of years with great success. The key is simply disciplining yourself to do it. Try it, you will like it!

Summary and Action Plan

1. Give up the Worry Habit today. Worry is a destructive way of using your vast mental power.

2. The most important things in your life are beyond your ability to plan or worry about. Infinite intelligence has a thousand ways to bring you your good, and it often isn't the way you expected! Isn't it great that you don't have to be limited to your own mind?

3. Stress normally doesn't come from a particular event, but rather your response to that event. Change your response and the stress will dissolve.

Exercise:

Use the A/B stress reduction technique to dissolve stress in any area of your life that is bothering you. Make sure to go through all five steps listed in the chapter. You will only succeed in dissolving the stress if you go into your mind and vividly recreate the experience. Just casual thinking about it won't work for you.

Chapter 17

Boost Your Brain Power

You are a genius! You have billions of brain cells, trillions of synaptic connections in your brain. You have at your disposal the most powerful, magical instrument of creation in this Universe! Most scientists agree, however, that we use only a small percentage of our real potential.

Marion Diamond, a highly respected professor at the University of California at Berkeley has done a tremendous amount of research on the human brain. Her studies have proven that we have tremendous untapped potential. See the book she co-authored with Janet Hopson: *Magic Trees of the Mind: How to Nurture Your Child's Intelligence, Creativity, and Healthy Emotions from Birth through Adolescence* (1998). This book contains resources and ideas for brain stimulation.

First, she showed that our brains really do not decline during most of our life. She carefully analyzed the research that was done in the 1950s where it had been concluded that we are constantly losing brain cells. She found out that *errors* were made in those studies. Most people lose very little (if any) of their mental abilities as they age (barring some disease).

Second, and even more exciting, she discovered that the human brain can actually *grow, and develop* during our lifetime if proper stimulation is applied. The cortex can actually grow in thickness, and in complexity.

Marion Diamond's research proves that we have tremendous power to mold and shape the very evolution of our own brain. We can literally cause our brain to grow, and develop much like our muscles.

This is why it is so important to feed positive thoughts and attitudes into your mind. You really can develop your mind and your mental capabilities!

Stimulate Your Mind

One of the best ways to keep your brain developing is to continue to expose yourself to new, and stimulating environments.

Travel Regularly–The Amazing Tonic

Travel has been compared to a powerful vitamin that revitalizes and restores vigor to a person. The simple fact is that when we travel to different locations our entire mind and body is exposed to a radically different set of stimuli. This can trigger great creativity in a person.

Additionally, traveling broadens our minds, and opens us to greater possibilities. Research indicates that when we travel to new areas we literally stimulate parts of our brain that may normally be unused. In this way we often trigger creative ideas that we can use in all parts of our minds.

Take every opportunity to travel in foreign countries. It is wonderful to hear the foreign language, and be exposed to the differences in culture. When you return home you will be amazed how you approach your life with greater creativity.

Learn a Foreign Language

Unfortunately, most people born in the U.S. have very little foreign language experience. Yet, if you can learn a foreign language there are several benefits.

First, it opens up entirely new areas you can travel to and feel competent in. Second, it stimulates your brain in new ways. Whenever you make an effort to speak in a foreign language it opens you to the thought and system of thinking of the particular culture.

Consider, for example that in Spanish the way you say "I forgot," is "se me olvido," which literally translated means: "it forgot itself to me." Think about the difference in world view when you say that as opposed to "I forgot." Which one encourages taking responsibility for your actions? Every language has many ideas born within it. Did you know that the Japanese language has no word for "love?"

For most people living in the United States, Spanish is an excellent language to learn. I frequently travel in Latin America, and am always reminded that the majority of this continent speaks Spanish. There is a wide variety and richness of culture in Latin America that is unknown to most U.S. citizens.

You can buy foreign language tapes and learn while you are driving to work. They are available many places! Wouldn't that be a creative use of your commute time? Just think of how much you could learn in one year of commuting!

Try learning a foreign language–you won't regret it!

Learn to Use a Computer

We are incredibly fortunate to be living at a time when computers become more powerful, cheaper and easier to use each year. There are now many programs that are so automated that they are extremely easy to use. The software is cheaper than ever. It is just as inexpensive to get a computer as a good TV and VCR.

Have you ever noticed that everyone seems able to buy a TV and VCR? If you desire to get a computer you can do it also. If you want to save even more money, buy a used computer. Computers that are only two years old can be bought for as little as $2-300. They may be slower, but can still perform word processing and other important computing functions.

A computer is nothing more than a brain IQ booster. The computer is to the brain what glasses are to the eyes. If you are near sighted as I am, and put on glasses, suddenly you can see things you would otherwise have missed out on. A whole new world opens up to you. The same is true of computing. As you learn to use a computer, you will discover that your effectiveness can rise dramatically. You will find that you can stay on top of vastly greater bodies of information.

In the world we are in today your success tomorrow depends on learning the computer today! Don't delay. Your future is at stake.

Use the Internet, Connect with Other People!

We are living in the most exciting time the world has ever known. Today you can connect to the Internet for about $20 per month and have conversations with people all over the world for the cost of a local call!

There was a severe earthquake in Japan recently. The same day I had communications with people in Japan and got direct information as to the actual conditions there. What a revelation that was. Instant communications with people thousands of miles away.

Whatever your interest area, there is probably a group on the Internet that is focused on it. You will find that your ability to grow in knowledge is accelerated by your ability to communicate with others of similar interests.

The other day I had a computer question I put on the Internet. I got back excellent answers from one man in Vancouver, Canada and another from the Netherlands! A global community has really been created. Make sure you are a part of it!

Learn Something New Every Day!

The other day my six-year-old came home from school and I asked him to tell me one thing he had learned for the day. Then it occurred to me that there is no reason as adults that we shouldn't be able to learn *at least* one new thing a day. Our mind has virtually unlimited ability to learn new things.

Whether the new information relates to your work, or a hobby, certainly there are things you can learn. Identify books, tapes or other resources available to you that can give you the information you need. There are many companies that have all kinds of programs on tape: books, motivational talks, language classes, whatever your interest is now available on a tape.

Increase Your Vocabulary

One of the easiest ways to increase your brainpower is to consistently increase your vocabulary. Just as learning a foreign language expands your mind, so does increasing your vocabulary. Did you know the vast majority of people confine themselves to a very small percentage of the language they speak?

Why not expand your knowledge of your language? You can become a cognoscenti – one who is knowledgeable. You will be surprised how much more successful you can be by just adding one or two words to your vocabulary per week. If you added two words per week, that would be over 100 words a year. Within 10 years you would have learned over 1,000 new words and, in the process, have greatly multiplied your ability to communicate well.

By the way, when you are using a word that may not be known by your listener, use a second clause that defines the first word. Notice where I used the word 'cognoscenti' in the previous paragraph. Do you see how I defined the word in the second part of the sentence? This is a comfortable way to use a larger vocabulary without embarrassing people that may not have your vocabulary. You actually are contributing to that person, too, because you are increasing his or her vocabulary as well.

Make use of Your Public Library

We have a wonderful public library system available in this country. For no charge, you have access to huge amounts of information. The greatest thinkers, the greatest inventions and ideas are waiting for you for free at your public library. Today most public libraries have video libraries where you can check out tapes on many subjects. If you want to do something chances are that there is a video or book waiting to give you step by step instructions.

Librarians are trained to help you get what you need. Don't be afraid to ask them for help. They are highly trained professionals, hoping that someone like you will come in whom they can assist in learning. Remember that the information you need to make your dream a reality is probably sitting right this second at your local public library. Go access it and get started in making your dream happen.

Stimulation Reduces Chance of Alzheimer's Disease

A study was recently performed on nuns in a convent to see which nuns preserved their mental capabilities as they aged, and which ones suffered from Alzheimer's or other age related problems. It was discovered that the nuns who kept their minds active, even doing such simple things as crossword puzzles, had a much lower incidence of Alzheimer's disease.

It turns out that the more we can stimulate our brain, the more connective nerve cells generate, which also provides us with protection in the event that some deterioration occurs. This is why any new activity that stimulates you with things that you don't do all the time, or requires you to learn will have positive effects on both your brain performance and longevity.

Reading this book is exposing you to many new ideas. If you follow through with the exercises you will be giving a direct stimulant to your brain that can only result in good for you.

Brain Stimulation May Cause you To Live Longer

In another study by Marion Diamond, one group of rats were placed in a highly stimulating environment. The other group was left in a cage with no stimulation. The highly stimulated rats lived to the human equivalent of 90 years, and their brains were substantially more developed than the other group. They had new glial cells, and enhanced connections between the different parts of the brain.

In short, the highly stimulated rats became smarter and lived longer. Does that suggest anything to you? Why not go out and pursue your dreams? Why not dare to become all you can be? You will probably live longer, become smarter, and have more fun.

Summary and Action Plan

1. Remember that your brain has vast untapped capabilities. The more you use your brain, the more effective it will become. Your brain can actually grow during your entire life. If you want to be more intelligent, start today.

2. Consciously choose to expose yourself to new ideas, and stimulating environments. This will develop your brain, reduce the chance of Alzheimer's, and extend your life.

3. One of the easiest ways to stimulate your brain is to learn a new subject such as a foreign language. This will greatly increase your options in life. Consider learning by tape in your car!

4. Travel whenever you can. Seek out new areas where the culture, foods and habits are different. Expose yourself to different world views. This will greatly broaden your world view and your awareness of your own life.

Exercise: *Use your journal to create a section for "New topics to learn." Put on your favorite music. Relax and enjoy the process.*

A. Think of three different subjects or skills that you would like to learn or increase your knowledge about. This could be a new language, a new computer skill, learning about a part of the world that interests you, or learning to speak before groups. Anything that you want to explore is perfect.

B. Identify one step that you could take in the direction of learning these new areas. Is there a tape available? Perhaps you will have to go the library and do some research. Maybe you could begin preparing for a trip to a new location.

C. Every night before you go to bed stop and notice whether you have made some progress on at least one of these topic areas. Make a notation in your journal under the new topic section to indicate which topic you have been focusing on. It can be one or more, but should always be at least one.

D. Whenever you think of a new topic that you would like to learn, put it down in your "New Topics to Learn" section of your journal. This way, you will always be working on a curriculum of higher learning. Whether you have gone to school or not doesn't matter. What <u>does</u> matter is that you keep using your mind to acquire new information! Eventually you will be highly educated.

Chapter 18

Give Up Your Addictions Forever!

Take control of your life! A prosperous life is a life free from addictions. What is an addiction, after all, but a behavior that is different from what you want, a behavior that you continue even though you wish to give it up?

There is a great empowerment that comes when you take control of your life and give up addictive behavior. You can be free of addictions, leaving behind unwanted behaviors, habits, and even emotional responses. It can be much easier than you ever imagined.

The approach I will share with you here has worked for many people with amazing simplicity and effectiveness. I certainly encourage you to use any other systems that you have found effective as well.

Step 1, Realize There are No addictions, only Choices!

If you really wish to be free from unwanted habits, you must first admit that the reason you have not yet given them up is *because you don't want to. In truth there are no addictions, there are only choices!*

Let me give an example in my own life. For many years I drank coffee. Like most people, I experienced a very pleasant feeling of high energy caused by the caffeine. But then I started noticing that it made me irritable, upset, and more anxious. It left me feeling listless and slightly depressed.

I frequently thought it would be better not to drink the coffee, but then I would find myself thinking about the caffeine rush, the sense of well being. The next thing I knew, I was drinking a cup of coffee. Then like clockwork, about 48 hours later, I would get a headache that would last a day. I even tried to figure out which pain relievers would be most effective to prevent the headache.

Then I started practicing complete self-honesty. I admitted that the reason why I drank the coffee was for the positive rush–but that I was also choosing to have the headache as well. Gradually, as I drank the coffee I became more and more aware that I was choosing the headache just as surely as I was choosing the caffeine rush.

Step 2, Give Up Self-Judgment and Observe Yourself Honestly

In order to honestly face our own choices, including some of the unpleasant side effects, we must be willing to give up self-judgment. For example, with my coffee drinking, I didn't judge or condemn myself simply because I was choosing to inflict a headache upon myself. I just observed the cause and effect relationship of the coffee drinking and the subsequent headache.

This is the key to becoming free. Simply be extremely honest with yourself about the effects of your behavior. Give up all self-judgment or condemnation. Gradually you will become completely aware of what you are doing. You will cease suppressing from your mind the consequences of your behavior.

Step 3, Make A Fully Conscious Decision

Once you have observed yourself for a period of time–without any self-judgment–your mind will begin to be much more aware of the full consequences of the behavior you are choosing. In my case what started to happen is that I realized I really didn't want the headaches and bad moods associated with caffeine.

From a position of non-judgment you will be surprised how easy it is to make a decision about what you want. You may decide you want to continue the particular behavior, and that the side effects are worth it. In fact, for me there was a period where I decided the headaches were an acceptable tradeoff for the stimulation the caffeine brought me.

The secret in making a fully conscious decision is that you are not deceiving yourself, nor are you trying to force a particular outcome on yourself. Rather, you are simply deciding *what you really want to do!*

This is the entire purpose of this process. It allows you to make an informed, self-honest decision about whether you wish to continue or discontinue a certain behavior.

Remember that there is only choice. Whatever you do is a choice, and your choice is neither good nor bad. It just has consequences! When you are clear about the consequences of your behavior, your decision will become much easier for you.

Step 4, Make a Commitment for a Particular Time Period

If you do decide to change your behavior, it is easiest to set a specific time period to try out your new choice. This offers two benefits. First, it gives a period of time to adjust to the new behavior (freedom from the addictive behavior). Second, it makes it easier to make the decision. The human mind is very strange about time. If you say you are giving up something forever, the mind may feel unsure, and perceive the task as overwhelming.

On the other hand, if you set up a period of time that appears realistic and is not overwhelming, you will find it easy to make the decision. In my coffee example, I decided to give up coffee on my birthday for one year. That seemed like a long enough period of time to really move beyond coffee, and yet not so long that it didn't give me the option of drinking it again if I wanted to.

Remember that this approach is based on being non-judgmental about the behavior. You may want to continue your habit, or not–and both choices are okay. After all, you are a mature, empowered human being. You can make whatever choice you feel is appropriate.

Once I made the decision to give up coffee for a year, it was amazingly simple to carry forward. You see, I was very clear that I wanted to make this choice. I knew that I would carry it out and would not waver. Why? Because no one made me make the choice, it was made of my own free will without any judgment whatsoever.

I found that having made this decision, coffee lost all temptation for me. Since I knew I wasn't going to drink any of it, then I no longer went through the process of deciding whether I should have a cup of coffee, with all of the temptation involved. That entire process was simply cut out of my mind. I had made my decision, and knew I was going to keep it.

That is the secret of this technique. When you decide to change your behavior, think carefully about the decision for as long as you want before you make it. Don't make it lightly, or based on other people's recommendations. Make the decision only because *you* want to.

Then, having made the decision–since it is your decision, based on a fully informed, fully clear analysis–you will find it is very easy to keep it. Most of the time when we find it difficult to keep our commitments, we are trying to give up something because we think we "should," not because we have decided to of our own volition.

I first tried this with coffee several years ago, and have had no difficulty in keeping my commitment. Every year on my birthday I decide whether I want to renew the commitment. If so, then I write it down in my journal.

You can experiment with changing all sorts of behaviors this way. Be very flexible with the time period. Sometimes I have made commitments for only 30 days because I am unsure whether

I really want to change the behavior or not. Choose a period you are comfortable with!

Experiment With the System

Once I discovered how powerful and easy it was to change behaviors with this system, I started using it for things not normally considered addictions. Consider these areas you could try this system:

Stop Criticizing your Spouse!

Many people get into an addictive pattern of attacking their spouse, and finding fault. This becomes so ingrained that it often leads to divorce. Consider stopping all criticism for some period of time that you know you can fulfill. You will be amazed at what happens–you will find so much peace in your relationship, there is a good chance you won't want to return to your old ways.

By the way, you may be thinking that you need to get your spouse to do this. But if you do it yourself, and stick with it, there is a good chance your spouse will change automatically.

Give up Fault-Finding!

It is so easy to get into a habit of finding fault in everyone and everything. We can see fault in politicians, in our friends, our family, the economy or virtually any area of life.

Yet it is critical that we learn to transform this habit, because we create according to our dominant thought patterns. Therefore, if we wish to find a world that is happy, positive, and moving into the future we want, we must learn to give up the addiction of fault-finding. Try this for a period of time; dare to give up fault finding and see what happens in your life.

Give up Self-Contempt!

So many people live in terrible judgment upon themselves. They never live up to their own expectations. They always feel they should be something different than they are. Try practicing total self-acceptance for a month, or two months, without any self-criticism! You will find that peace begins to come into your world. As you learn to accept yourself, you will find miracles start flowing into your world.

Choose Your Ideal Weight

I have used this system with remarkable effectiveness to set my weight. After we had our first child, for some reason I put on about 15 pounds and never was able to take it off. In fact I kept getting heavier. I tried several diets with the same results: I would lose the weight and put it back on again. A very familiar story, I am sure you will agree.

Finally, at the beginning of the year I made a commitment, a fully informed choice regarding the weight I wanted to be. I didn't commit to eating, or not eating any particular foods. I committed only that by a certain date I would be a certain weight, with a several pound margin of error built in.

Somehow, since that time, knowing that it was my choice, without any *should's* involved, I have lost over 15 pounds, and kept the weight off. What is really interesting is that it has been effortless. I haven't been on a diet. All that has happened is that I have really become aware of the effect different foods have on my body. I naturally have tended to eat less fats, and less food in general.

The process has been so effortless. But the real secret, I am sure, is that within my heart I knew I would lose the weight. I didn't doubt because I made the commitment and knew I would keep it. After all, we can all lose weight if we have to. It is just a matter of choice.

That is the fundamental point of this whole chapter. All behaviors are choices. If you simply can view all the choices you are making without judgment, then you will be free to make decisions that are most effective and serve your life the best. After all, it is your life. However you want to be is okay. It will have consequences, but it is okay. Relax, and choose the life you really want! You can do it!

Summary and Action Plan

1. The key to mastering your addictions is choice. You can give anything up if it really is your choice to do so.

2. The key to remember is that we have no indecision or difficulty if we have really made up our minds. Temptation doesn't arise unless you are considering changing your mind. This is why you want to set a period you are comfortable with. You will be amazed at how easy it is to follow through since doubt will never enter your mind.

3. Give up all self-judgment. Remember that it is perfectly okay to engage in smoking or other habits, <u>but the habit may have very bad health consequences!</u> You are not bad if you continue with an addiction, but you may end up paying a price that is unpleasant for you and your loved ones.

4. Self-honesty is the key. What do you really want? Why do you want to change? Is it because someone else wants you to? Are you experiencing negative consequences in your life? Follow your own heart, and you can release any addiction.

Exercise:

A. Once you are absolutely clear that you want to release a habit or behavior, choose some time period wherein you will cease the behavior.

B. Choose a period that you are comfortable with. If smoking were your choice, start with 30 days, and then before the 30 days has expired, renew for another 30 days if that is what you want. This leaves choice in your hands.

C. Put your agreement in writing and review it each morning during your time period. Write a list of other behaviors you would like to change and try this system for periods that you find comfortable.

Chapter 19

Reality Check: How to Deal with Adversity

You can count on great success, and increase in your peace, happiness and well being. But as long as you and I are having a human experience there will be times when things turn out differently than we expect.

There will be other times when we don't fulfill our own expectations. This is nothing to fear or to worry about. Within you and I there is a built-in ability to overcome these moments, to begin anew, and to create wonderful new opportunity. The secret is to snap out of the hypnotic spell of limitation and realize that you must proclaim your power, your right to be victorious at every moment. Then the mists of negativity will dissolve in the brilliant sun of your faith.

If the Winds of Adversity Blow, Trim Your Sail

Did you know that at one time in history sail boats could only sail in the direction of the prevailing wind? If the wind blew west, you sailed west. If it blew north, you sailed north. You could vary a little bit from the wind's direction, but in general you had to go the way the wind blew.

But in 1700s a great invention occurred. The sloop was invented, with a sail that could be trimmed. This permitted a sailboat to sail almost directly into the wind. This brought a great revolution in sailing. Suddenly boats could travel even when the winds blew in unfavorable directions!

All you have to do with a modern sailboat to sail towards the wind is to pull in the boom, trim your sail, and suddenly you can sail in almost any direction! You can do the same thing with any condition that occurs in your life. Instead of resigning yourself to a negative outcome, you can pull in your sail and transform it into good.

Look Beyond the Appearance

The sailors of old saw a wind blowing in the wrong direction and just assumed it wouldn't take them where they wanted to go. They were right until more creative sailors came along later, and refused to limit themselves by the direction the wind was blowing. So you, too, must learn to see opportunity where others see only limitation.

We have discussed in numerous places in this book that true success is learning to see opportunity and possibilities where others see only defeat. No matter what you may think, no matter how things appear, you must deeply hold onto the conviction that good and only good will come to you out of it.

I can give you a simple example of transforming a negative into a positive that recently occurred in my office. In my office we are totally dependent on properly functioning computers. Our clients demand immediate service and often are under great pressure.

A few weeks ago I decided to upgrade one of my computers. My computer consultant came, made the change and everything seemed fine–for about two days. Then suddenly everything started to go haywire. Things went from bad to worse. The main server that contained all the data became corrupted, which meant I had to restore data from other sources. Then another machine failed at the same time. Suddenly, out of six computers, two were not functioning, including the most important one.

We were frantic. Clients don't want to hear that the computers are not working. That line only will take you so far! After working on the computers for about two weeks, without any success in getting them working right again, I stepped back and decided there must be some good, some miracle waiting to come from this seeming disaster.

I went into my office, and became very quiet. I calmly proclaimed all things to be in divine order, and trusted that good–and only good would–come forth. I confess that up until that time I had not maintained complete calm, in fact I had become immersed in the drama of it all, becoming upset and angry.

But when I stopped, became quiet, and proclaimed a blessing, a chain of events transpired that still seems miraculous to me. I finally decided that I could no longer remain with the operating system I was using; that we were investing too much time in a bad system. So instead I decided to redo the whole system. That was a high-risk decision since the new system was untested with our machines and software. But I felt a sense of inner peace about it all. I asked my prayer support group to ask for a blessing on my computers.

That weekend I spent over 20 hours with my computer consultant redesigning the system. By the end of the weekend our machines were running better than I had ever seen them. They were twice as fast, totally stable, and much easier to use. When Monday morning rolled around my secretaries couldn't believe how much better everything was running.

Here is the point: I probably would have remained with the old outdated system if I weren't forced into making the upgrade. But when I stopped, became calm and blessed the conditions, the answer became obvious and the means were made available. The result was fantastic. In other words, what appeared to be a disaster was really an enormous blessing.

This is the golden key to overcoming appearances. Bless them, and trust that good is rushing to you at this very moment. Remain open, trust, and good will come to you.

Persist, for Your Good is Waiting for You!

All through this book you have seen example after example of people who persisted and created great success. Edison stands out as a great example of this principle. There is another true story that will remind you to always persist.

About 90 years ago, a man invested his entire life savings into special gold mining equipment. He came west, bought land, and began mining. Unfortunately, he didn't find the gold he was searching for right away, became discouraged, and finally decided to sell out. He sold his land, and everything on it for pennies on the dollar.

The man who bought the mine had the dirt analyzed, and concluded that gold probably was there, but was deeper down. So he started mining again. In less than 10 feet he found an incredibly rich vein of gold. He became an instant millionaire, and supplied prosperity to many people. All because he was willing to persist in the face of difficulty.

This story should remind you that the gold you seek is probably right in front of you. Be willing to find it; be willing to dig deeper. You will be richly rewarded for your efforts!

Remember, the gold you seek may be just around the corner. Don't stop now!

Begin Again!

Suppose you find yourself angry, despondent or upset, as I felt when my computers were broken down. There is no reason to become angrier with yourself for losing control. Instead, you can stop and calmly assess what has occurred. Notice carefully how you are responding to the circumstances. Is your response helping or hurting?

If you have to, leave your office for a few minutes, or change your environment in some other way. But whatever you do, stop and become calm. Within you lies a resource, a power to begin again, no matter what you are facing. And when you do begin again, you magically will begin to see answers where once you saw only problems.

The secret is to remain gentle and forgiving of yourself and others. With this spirit you can always start over, and usually can get a much better result than you ever obtained. Life is very forgiving if you can just maintain the right attitude.

Summary and Action Plan

1. If you encounter an event, or experience that seems negative, stop, bless it, name it as good, trust that good is going to come from it.

2. Trim your sails by adopting a positive attitude. This will permit you to transform what would be a negative event into a positive experience.

3. Refuse to believe in the appearance of negativity or failure. Persist until you find success. Remember that the gold you seek is probably right in front of you!

4. If you feel you have failed in some way don't get too serious about it. Stop, become peaceful. Forgive yourself and all others. Then begin again. There is a magic power of transformation within you that will move you ahead to even greater success as long as you release the past, and trust in the future.

Exercise:

A. Write out any areas you feel you have failed, or at least not attained the success you desired.

B. Forgive yourself and any others involved.

C. Declare in your mind that you release the outcome of your actions to the highest and best good. By doing this you release your creative power to begin again, and surely you move towards a future better than you could have ever imagined.

Chapter 20

Enjoy the Healing Power of Integrity and Forgiveness!

If you really want to walk the high road and live a life of exceptional joy, peace and prosperity, you will want the twin healing powers of integrity and forgiveness. Integrity, to steer and guide you along the road in your life. Forgiveness of yourself and others when you feel you have made a mistake. One cannot exist without the other, for we are imperfect beings living in an imperfect world.

Be True to Yourself

Each of us has very different standards and beliefs about what is right. The great secret of integrity is that you must find out the truth by looking at your own inner experience. Integrity is not simply following some set of pre designed rules. Rules are simply someone else's ideas of what is right in a given situation. But some of the worst injustices in the world have been done by people "following the rules."

Real integrity requires looking to the underlying ethics of the circumstances. Are your actions going to hurt someone? Is your failure to act, even though within the rules, going to hurt someone? What are the relative merits and needs of all concerned?

As you learn to see yourself as a being with great power, capable of manifesting miraculous outcomes, you will see how important it is to use your power with honesty, integrity and concern for all.

When you understand that you are drawing off an inexhaustible source of love, wisdom and prosperity, then you will see that attempting to take from others, to deceive, really is contrary to your highest and best interests.

But always you must test out your conduct in the sacred dimension of your own conscience and heart. After all, on your last day on Earth, it is you and you alone that will decide whether your life has been well lived. Better that you feel satisfied with your life than to constantly compromise yourself.

Consider the ethics of the family that sheltered Ann Frank from the Nazis during World War II. The family secretly hid this Jewish girl from the authorities. They broke the conventional ethical rules by lying, by not respecting the authorities in place. Yet who can doubt that they were in fact operating from a much higher sense of integrity?

You see, had they been of small mind and character, they might have felt they had no choice but to be honest citizens and turn her in. Many of their countrymen did just that. But instead they considered all the consequences, the value of human life, and honored their own sense of inner integrity. Surely their attempt to shelter her was morally right.

And so it always is. We must look within to all circumstances to determine what is really ethical, what is really right. Then we must act to the best of our ability in this way. As we do this a great inner peace will descend upon us.

You Will Have as Much Power As You can Trust Yourself With

The power you have to manifest miracles will rise in direct proportion to the degree of self-trust, and self-acceptance that you have. If you fear success, fear power, and feel that inwardly you are a bad person, you will keep yourself small and impotent. But as you begin to feel comfortable with yourself, with your own values, with your own integrity, you will open the floodgates to power.

For you are the gatekeeper to your own power. You are the one who decides what to think, what to feel about all things. It is you that passes judgment upon yourself. It is you that dispenses forgiveness as well.

It is always you that watches your own behavior. You are the one that knows whether you keep your commitments. You know your true nature. Yet for many people there is an inner fear of how and what you truly are. Somewhere within lies the lingering fear that if you had great power you would be corrupted, that you would act in a way that is contrary to your highest good.

As long as that inner doubt persists, as long as you think that you are unworthy of power, then in that exact measure you will deny yourself that power. But as you begin to trust yourself, as you begin to discover you are good and worthy of the best that life has to offer, you will see your outer life becoming ever richer and more vibrant.

As your inner trust grows, you will find that people are drawn to you. For as you trust yourself, so others will also trust you. This will empower you in every part of business and personal endeavors. What business can proceed without complete integrity, complete trust? All lasting success must be founded on these qualities.

But this trust will only arise in you if you act in accordance with your own values! You must learn to see what you really feel about things and then live in accordance with those inner beliefs. Again, it is worth repeating that the values you should aspire towards need not be those that others would put upon you, but they must be your own values, based on your own world view.

Forgiveness, the Great Liberator!

Forgiveness is your great ally, the lubricant on the road of life that permits us to move forward. Every human being makes mistakes. The question is how to view these mistakes in our lives, and in the lives of those that touch our world. The way that we habitually respond will have a tremendous, long lasting impact on our lives.

For example, if two people divorce (and I have worked with thousands of people getting divorced) they can either treat each other with respect and forgiveness, or they can harbor resentments for years, or in some cases a whole lifetime. I have seen couples that won't talk, and make the lives of their children a hell for decades. Why do they do this? Who really wins? Who loses?

It is obvious that their children lose. But what is not so obvious is that they themselves lose by their unwillingness to forgive and move on. Forgiveness is the great healer; it permits people to free up that part of the mind that is associated with an event or person, and move onto better creations.

As long as a person withholds forgiveness that person has to hold onto bitterness or anger in their own mind (regardless of how justified it is). That lack of forgiveness will slowly eat away at the fabric of the person's mind and life. Bitterness, anger and hatred simply consume our life force, causing us to become sick, to become unhappy.

I once heard a speaker say very correctly that she forgives everyone in her life, not for them, but for her own health and well being! She went on to explain that the person that gets sick from bitterness, from lack of forgiveness is not the person at whom the anger is directed, but instead is the person who will not forgive!

Forgiveness should be extended to all people who have touched our lives. For we know not what their destiny is, their reason for being. At the same time, we should grant to ourselves the same dispensation of forgiveness, continually and liberally. For we know all too well our own shortcomings, our own failures.

If you have any judgment or anger that you are holding onto regarding your own life, let it go–forgive it, release it. It can only do you harm. You cannot change your past. All you can do is release it and trust that somehow that the Supreme Intelligence of the world can transform your act into good.

As you learn to forgive yourself, to be loving of yourself, you will find that your measure of self-trust increases, your power increases, your good increases. As you forgive others you will find your friendships increase, your success multiplies and your life becomes ever happier.

The choice is yours, why not start living and walking the high road today, the road to a life with integrity, self-trust and forgiveness! You can do it!

Summary and Action Plan

1. Learn to look within your own heart, your own feelings, to determine what you believe is right. Then do your best to live within this integrity.

2. As you begin to live with ever greater integrity, you will find that self trust builds up in your life. Your self-trust will in turn lead to greater integration of your power, and you will find your success building dramatically. Success in human relationships, success in business, success in inner peace.

3. Remember that mistakes are normal for all human beings. Learn to forgive yourself on a daily basis, and forgive all others who have interacted with you. Start each day newly, with no judgments, no angers, no resentments. Start looking for a new life and you will find it.

4. Remember that forgiveness heals you, and prevents you from getting sick. If you can't forgive for the sake of others, do it for your own sake. Whatever your motivation, learn to let go, and release people to their own destinies. It does you no good to hold on.

Exercise:

Sit quietly in a room, preferably with some soothing music on.

A. Take a piece of paper and list out all people that you feel have wronged you, or that you are unhappy with.

B. List all the people that you feel you have wronged, or failed to treat properly.

C. One by one, go through the list of people that you believe have wronged you; forgive, and release them. Ask in your prayers that they be blessed, and that their destiny be good. Remember, as you ask for another, so you will receive in your own life. This is how you will know if you have truly forgiven: if you can ask that good come to them in the name of God.

Once you have released a person to God, then you are leaving his/her destiny up to God– which is where it belongs. Keep going over the list until you feel inner peace regarding your release of these people.

D. Now go down the list of people that you think you have wronged. One by one ask in your mind that they forgive you. You don't have to speak to the people, although it certainly cannot hurt to do so. Ask, and accept forgiveness and release for each of these people. Ask that God's will and good come to these people.

E. Keep going over your forgiveness list until you feel inner peace.

F. Before you go to bed each day, forgive everyone who has touched your life, and ask for forgiveness for any way you may have fallen short. Then release the day to its divine perfection and move on to a good night's sleep. The next day you will awaken refreshed and ready to start anew, free from past restrictions, angers and resentments.

Chapter 21

Walk Into a Wonderful Future!

Much of this book has been dedicated to supplying you with the tools to attain your individual dream in life, to live a truly prosperous life. This chapter is dedicated to the manifestation of a joint dream for all people, a future that we can all walk into with anticipation, happiness and confidence.

We have talked about the power of visualization, and that there are answers to all things if we are just willing to persist. These principles can be applied globally, as well as individually. There is no problem facing this wonderful earth that you and I, together, cannot resolve.

In recent years, especially in the United States, a climate of pessimism has arisen in many people, an attitude that a decline in the standard and quality of life is inevitable. A fearful attitude towards changes in the country and the world exists in the minds of many people.

The constant focusing of the various media on the problem spots reinforces this attitude. This serves to push people into fear thinking, rather than solution thinking. We can turn this around by focusing on the following points.

We Are Living in the Most Peaceful Time Man Has Known!

In many ways, today is the most peaceful, productive time the planet earth has ever known. Every era of human history has had wars, violence, and plagues as well. Yet today, we have large numbers of people living together in relative peace.

Consider that the United States has living within its borders over 250 million people that have been able to govern themselves peacefully, without internal warfare for over 140 years. Not long ago the entire planet earth had less than 200 million people, so in reality within this one country we have created a world at peace! If we can do that with one country this large, it can be done with the whole world!

Your Likelihood of Living a Long, Healthy and Safe Life is Better Now than Ever Before

Because the media constantly focuses on problems to the exclusion of everything else, many people get a distorted picture of life. In reality, the average person today has a better chance to live a long, healthy, safe life than people did 50 or 100 years ago.

In the past, the average family lost at least one of their children as they were growing up. This was a reason why it was so important to have large families. Many women died in childbirth. Countless people died at early ages due to incurable diseases. And, of course, the U.S. had the bloodiest, highest casualty war, the Civil War, over 100 years ago.

Today, even with some of the health and crime problems we have, our problems are considerably less than existed in the past. This is why the average person still has a better chance to live a long life today.

So to put it very simply, there has never been a safer time to live on the planet, on an average! This is the truth, yet if you watch media you would never believe it.

Opportunity for Global and Individual Prosperity Has Never Been Greater!

For the first time in human history, we have at our disposal tools that can end world hunger, control population growth, and dramatically improve the quality of all life. In the past, there were times when it appeared as though a good, prosperous life had to be something for the few, while the majority were restricted to lives of struggle and poverty.

Today, with our wonderful technological advances, we can create abundant food supplies for all people. We can make advances in the treatment of disease much more rapidly due to the global communications network. When problems arise we have tools and communication skills to deal with them.

The Greatest Inventions, the Most Glorious Improvements in the Quality of Life are Yet to Come

We must be careful not to slip into the same limited thinking pattern that leads people into pessimism and hopelessness. It is easy to succumb to the mass belief that perhaps the best has already occurred, and the future holds little to be excited about.

But the creative force in the human spirit has just begun to unfold to its greatest potentials. Undoubtedly, the greatest inventions, leading to the greatest liberation of the human race are yet to come. Anti-aging medications, safe, non-polluting, abundant energy sources, unlimited fresh water are just a few of the innovations that will be coming very soon. Other things are so far beyond our perception we would have difficulty even grasping them, as would people 100 years ago if they could view today.

War and Violence Really Can End

Most of us have been programmed from the time we were children to believe that war and violence will always exist because that is just the way people are. This message comes to us from so many different sources that it is hard to even conceive that world peace and prosperity is possible, and coming.

Yet for thousands of years people also believed that man would never fly, and that to even dream of this was irresponsible. Until, of course, the Wright brothers (among others) proved that flying was possible. So it will be with war and violence. The majority may continue to believe it is foolish even to dream of a world where joyous freedom and peace prevails. But a small minority of people will hold onto this dream until they manifest it into reality!

It doesn't take many people to change the world. It only takes a few that are dedicated and have mastered the power of their own minds. With this power focused and dedicated to the highest good, amazing miracles can unfold in a very short period of time.

Change Can Occur Immediately!

We are used to thinking of change occurring very gradually over long periods of time. Actually, major changes often occur very quickly. Scientists studying evolution now believe that a species would stay very similar for a long period of time, and then suddenly would make a dramatic change.

Certainly there are many examples in the human race of changes that have occurred simultaneously in various parts of the world without any intercommunication occurring. Virtually every major scientific breakthrough has popped up in various places, with various scientists, at almost the same time.

For example, Darwin's theory of evolution was being developed in England at the same time that the theory was being developed in a number of other countries, without any communication going on between the parties.

You are Part of the Answer if You So Choose!

Each of us has the inalienable choice of what we will dedicate our life to. If you would like to see a world that we can proudly leave to our children, then start visualizing such a world. Start seeing a world that is a safe, peaceful, exciting place to live in.

Start expecting that this is coming into reality much faster than you ever imagined. See answers coming forth for all sorts of problems that face societies: political answers, economic answers, social answers, and health answers.

See and feel a wonderful sense of excitement coming forth–literally bursting forth–in many places across the earth. Sense the excitement building; a sense that an entirely new beginning is at hand, a chance to move this world into a higher, more glorious existence than we ever dreamed.

Are these realistic visions, or simple pipe dreams? I suggest to you that they are entirely true, and that the reason I am writing this book and you are reading it is because we are both committed to the same purpose. Why not believe in the best, most exciting future for all people? Give up the old ways, the negative ways, and welcome in the new. You will never regret it!

You Can Count On a Wonderful Future!

In this book we have covered many tools, many ideas for awakening your mind and spirit to your true human potential. You have vast potential to transform your life. The fact that you have chosen to persist and complete this book should indicate to your own mind that you are committed to a life of great happiness and fulfillment.

If you maintain that commitment, then you will unleash an immense power to transform your life into a wonderful, happy, divine experience. The choice is up to you, and you have already made it!

Dare to claim your future, a future that you and I can look forward to with great anticipation. A future of peace, prosperity, and wonderful innovations on every level. It will happen, because you have greatness in your soul!

Summary and Action Plan

1. You are living in the golden age of the human race, with the greatest opportunity that has ever been known to man.

2. You have a better chance of living an abundant, safe, prosperous life than ever before in human history.

3. The best is truly yet to come! Avoid any tendency to see the best times as having already past. The greatest inventions, the greatest advancements, the greatest spiritual attainments lie now and in your future.

4. You can be part of the answer to building a wonderful, happy, prosperous future for all people. You can dedicate yourself to living a life of joy, happiness, and service to the world. If you do this, your life will be better than you ever imagined!

Exercise:

A. Practice seeing the world as a wonderful place of opportunity.

B. Visualize people working together in peace, harmony and cooperation.

C. Develop an expectancy that good can come both to you and to the world in ways and methods greater than you could ever imagine.

Chapter 22

The Great Love

This book would not be complete without returning to your ultimate purpose in this life. Greater than any goal achieved is the attainment of supreme love, of eternal joy. To live in this world without knowing this joy is to miss the greatest gift of all. As Paul said in the New Testament, Love is the greatest of all things.

Within you at this very instant is an unspeakable joy, a supreme experience of who and what you really are. This experience is not some abstract idea about life; it is a living, real experience that will awaken within your own body and mind. You have nerves and sensations that you may never have experienced yet. When you have felt this great love, your life will never be the same again.

To know this great joy is like jumping into a sea of unending joy, a place where all things are known to you, all fear is dissolved. Ecstatic joy beyond all comprehension awaits you right this second. It is who you really are. You have become caught up in the story of your life, yet you have the ability to stop at any time and reconnect to your source. After all–it is your story!

If you wish to build a life of long lasting happiness, and ultimate success, you must be willing to ask for the kingdom, and be willing to be the ruler of your domain. You must be willing to have permanent and lasting happiness.

It takes great courage to live in happiness. It takes great courage to give up struggle, to give up suffering, to quit believing in their place in your life. Dare to become the incarnation of grace in this world. Only when you have fully assimilated your divine purpose, when you have remembered who you are, will you be free.

You must be willing to give up the widely held delusion that suffering is good, and turn your back on suffering once and for all. You must dare to live in real happiness. Not feigned happiness, not a mask covering inner sorrow. Real, true, complete happiness. This is what you must have the courage to create.

It is my prayer that as you read this, right this instant, you are given the experience of supreme joy. For any person who has drunk the nectar of divine bliss is never again the same. The rest of your days will be dedicated to the awakening of this grace in your life, and the life of those in your world.

You are the light of the world! Wherever you go your light shines and bestows a blessing on all. Awaken now to your destiny. It is a good destiny, a destiny of greatness. Greatness in receiving, greatness in giving. The adventure is just beginning: you will hardly recognize your life even a year from now. Wonderful good is coming to you now.

Let go! You have already crossed the threshold into a new life. Amazing good is rushing to you right now. New relationships, wonderful friends, new opportunities, radiant abundance of every good thing. All of this and more awaits you.

Awaken!

About the Author

Robert Sidell is one of five children. He now lives in the country with his wonderful wife, a menagerie of children, 6 dogs, 1 guinea pig and 20 chickens.

He has been a practicing attorney since 1977. He graduated from the University of California, Berkeley, with honors for academic excellence. He is admitted to practice law in California, Arizona and Nevada.

Shortly after becoming a lawyer, Robert had a spiritual awakening that caused him to see the world through new eyes. He realized at that time that this world has unlimited potential, and dedicated the rest of his life to sharing the truths that are contained in this book. He was ordained as a non denominational minister in 1984.

Robert believes that the future well being of this world depends upon a new level of spiritual awakening in the human race that will cause people to learn to honor each other beyond their religion, race, tradition or background.

He believes that we stand at a point of unique opportunity in the human race to take a major step forward spiritually, emotionally, and in every positive way. He has taught seminars for the last 15 years on these topics. If you are interested in learning more about this work you can reach him at:

702.384.3847
rbsidell@aol.com

NOTES

NOTES

NOTES